Maurice Gartshore

SECOND THOUGHTS.

Foreword.

I call this journal 'Second Thoughts' as a way of explaining my personal take on issues of the day which without a little scrutiny might pass unnoticed in the hurly-burly of life in the digital age. If there are any readers out there, some will perhaps nod, some will shake their heads, but as a grumpy old man I have tried very hard to justify my comments with evidence where necessary. I hope a little banter at times will lighten the gloom.

I have decided against the constriction that dates impose on journals. Too much guilt associated with missing a day when really nothing much happens, and thoughts take a holiday. I've used the weather to indicate the passage of time. I live in Scotland so my weather may seem at odds with yours.

1.

The last day of 2021. Clouds low, a sodden day of mist and drizzle.

If a year could be mirrored by weather this would be it. A year of masks and jags and the blithering idiocy of Boris Johnson. A slim year for me in the 'making' department. Little written or painted. I drift towards my computer when boredom or conscience pricks to further my flimsy language skills. Duo.

Spanish, German, French—the latter with more expectation that I can rattle through it. I complete the tasks and add to my store of words. If a Spaniard or a German were foolish enough to engage me in their language I'd flounder like a landed fish. Learning vocabulary does not a linguist make. Words are not language. Language is what happens when you apply rules to words. Without a knowledge of the rules you can only hope for a tenuous comprehension. Words are like the notes in music: without that indefinable magic that brings notes to life, they are only notes and stir no emotions. Music is what you do with notes and language (the music of it) is how you use the words. It is the line on which the washing hangs. Without the line or shall we say the rules of grammar and tenses no communication is possible but the occasional word which hangs hopeful but essentially useless in the air a moment and dies. I've now begun to read Animal Farm in German in the hope that such a task might offer other rewards. I'll stick at it in the hope that at some stage I may wander through a sentence without recourse to my dictionary. Gist will do me: I don't seek perfection.

Bishop Desmond Tutu has died. Interesting article in The Guardian mentioning the word 'Ubutu' which Tutu used. It has no easy meaning in English but seems to relate the individual's sense of self to his awareness of others. Coincidentally, two friends came for lunch yesterday and one told us his father's constant criticism of him was that 'he was always thinking about other people.' We all laughed. Don't suppose Margaret Thatcher would have got the joke.

If anyone gets Tutu's doctrine it would be Richard Holloway, the ex Primus of the Scottish Episcopal Church who went against its opposition to Gay Rights and granting the Priesthood to women, to forge his own path.

I'm reading Holloway's book 'The Heart of Things.' A collection of poems and prose that he uses as a basis to formulate his thoughts on melancholia, mourning, war, regret and forgiveness. He quotes Louis McNeice's beautiful poem 'Snow' as an example of how our perceptions of reality should be 'open' and later Derek Mahon's poem 'Yaddo, or 'A Month in the Country' written from the artists' retreat in Saratoga Springs New York to his two teenage children in England. It's a poem about regret and loss and one any divorced father who has lost touch with his children would recognise. (Own score: two in touch—

one not). I don't know Mahon's work but I need to read more. One of the gifts of reading is the way for me one book can lead to another. As an admirer of Holloway I'm happy to take his advice on what is worth reading. Jan Morris was another name mentioned and I've bought two of her books never having read her work. In fact, it's her book 'Thinking Again'—a daily diary of thoughts and recollections that has triggered this, my own, 'Thoughts.'

2.

A new year breaks windy and yet warm. Too warm?

Now that we're all conscious of global warming,

any perceived aberration in the weather is attributed

to G-W. Walked Izzy my dog up The Knock our local

hill. Twig litter everywhere and a reindeer rubbing his

antlers on a sizeable pine bough on the tennis court at the Hydro. You've got to hand it to The Hydro for originality. It's a family hotel and amusing the kiddies comes high on its list of priorities. A huge wooden castle, some donkeys, goats and alpacas on the far side of the hill.

Last night Martin and Annette came and after the countdown we ended up watching Two Weddings and a Funeral. Great fun as ever: Hugh Grant being Hugh Grant with all the loveable twitches and apologies that inevitably made his vulnerability a hit with the ladies. But it was Rowan Atkinson as the bumbling vicar at the wedding that took the biscuit, his nerves confusing the names of the bride and groom. With a face like Atkinson's you have to be funny and by God the man is.

Bed at two-thirty with a dog that was puzzled that she'd been denied three and half hours of her usual sleep. 'When you sleep, I sleep.'

Holloway's book again. Having recently watched footage of The Second World War and the carnage in men and materiel, I was struck by some lines in Louis McNeice's poem 'Prayer Before Birth' beginning 'I am not yet born' where he lists the possible future of such a one born into the world to suffer the slings and arrows of what it is to be human—a perceptive foetus if ever there was one. When you watch film of First World War soldiers marching (many smiling for the camera) to their probable deaths at The Front, McNeice's plea from the to-be-born that he might be filled…

'With strength against those who would freeze my humanity, would dragoon me into legal automaton,'… seems particularly prescient.

I couldn't help wondering why soldiers, presumably his 'automatons', unthinking, obedient to any order, so readily give themselves into the hands of maniacs like Adolf Hitler, to kill and despoil, when they are not themselves threatened. One can only assume their training so de-humanises that the self and normal benign humane impulses are subsumed by some imagined superior precept. Oh yes, I know they were conscripted, but I wonder sometimes what would happen if folk generally said, 'I'm not going, there's no point to it.' That Jews were depicted among the 'Untermensch' in Hitler's Aryan myth and the North Vietnamese as 'gooks' in Uncle Sam's struggle against communism makes their slaughter an act without blame or shame but rather a duty.

Of course, we are all a prey to the lies and deceptions of politicians and it takes a degree of intelligence to discern when one is being used. Why is it that the psychopaths, the narcissistic maniacs of this world rise to positions of such power that they are able to deceive so easily and drag ordinary men and women into such barbarity? Trump's followers stormed The Capitol at the urge to 'fight like hell' and as quickly turned on their heels when he told them to 'go home.' This in 2021. Have we learned nothing in a thousand years? As I write, Putin's forces are massing on the borders of Ukraine and only Putin knows what will happen next. One man will decide whether many will die or not. One man may again plunge the world into a self-destructive chaos.

Russia's age-old mistrust of The West, magnified in Putin's world view, manifests itself in a fear of Ukraine becoming a NATO member. What next would he have his people believe—that missiles will be directed at Moscow? Does wee Putin, in the final years of his rule, wish to reclaim previously held territories as a legacy —the narcissist appeased— or is it merely a gesture occasioned by genuine fear for the safety of his country? Soldiers fulfil the will of the leader. No doubt the Russian people are being fed his propaganda in the absence of any opposition, but then perhaps we are also being encouraged to believe that Western Europe is under threat from Russia. When the lies win, we will all die— innocent women and children blown …

'like thistledown hither and

thither'…

'like water held in the

hands… would spill…'

'Let them not make me a stone and let them not spill

me…' says McNeice.

I was amused by a recollection of Jan Morris

speaking of her days as a reporter being adjured by

an African politician to write about his country in an

amusing and readable way 'where possible

coinciding with the truth.' Is that how politicians

think?

As I write I'm listening to Viol Music for the Sun King

by the French composer Marin Marais who died in

1728. Again, I come clean and admit influence: I

bought this CD after watching 'Tous Les Matins du Monde' that stunningly beautiful French film set during the reign of Louis XIV. It shows Marin Marais looking back at his young life when he was a pupil of Monsieur de Sainte Colombes and it features the music of the period especially that for viol da gamba. I've always loved the sound of the cello, and this was even more sonorous. The instrument most akin to the tone of the human voice they say, and I believe it.

The light is going. It's four o'clock and the dimming spears of the cordyline are waving goodnight.

3.

Still a wind but the weather mild. Warmest January day in London in twenty years may please some but for me the perfect Winter day is cold with clear blue skies. It does seem that our seasons are losing their distinctive characteristics. Only television at Christmas feels the need for fake snow to remind us of the season. If they could afford a stagecoach with steaming team stopping at the inn, I'm sure they'd add that. Oh, and I wish they'd realise that the sight of a deciduous tree in full leaf in the background does suggest that the programme wasn't filmed in the depths of Winter. But that's TV for you—the eternal illusion played out for us all to enjoy. Has that celebrity talking to camera on the top of that mountain really climbed all the way? Did the camera really follow that young wildebeest among the herd of thousands through months of its journey? All lies are equal, but some lies are more serious than others: the Vox pop that interviews six shoppers to ask what they think of this or that can be edited to present what passes for a uniform view. Dangerous stuff, but it's there all the time and the less discerning are not aware of how their views can be manipulated. As I age, I'm finding that TV adverts increasingly puzzle me. What is that trying to get me to buy, I ask my partner Christine. And Christine, also aging, isn't quite sure. People walking through walls or flying through the air can be promoting house insurance or a cure for erectile disfunction. The links between product and some perceived psychological trigger encouraging purchase grow more tenuous by the day. And why is it believed by advertisers that a stuffed grizzly will persuade me to eat a particular yoghurt or a squirrel's advice on house purchase is sound?

Jan Morris touched on the modern phenomenon of 'algorithm' in her 'Thoughts' book. While she sought its derivation, I'm more interested in the sinister way in which my needs can be assumed from my purchases by a machine. Perhaps a dating site on which you strike up a conversation with Glenda Smith may decide that there are other Glenda's who might be of interest to you. 'Others who went to bed with

Glenda may also like to go to bed with Freda and Sarah and Naomi and Sheila…' who also have ginger hair and large breasts. Bugger their algorithms I say. Leave me alone to decide which way the wind of my desires may blow. And while we're at it, to hell with Facebook and all its stupidities. I do wonder what function this platform serves. Does it stimulate debate? No. You daren't demur. In the main it is a cosy wee tent which you share with your 'like-minded' chums in the garden lighting a candle and eating your mum's rock buns. Being prone to iconoclastic impulses I've been burned at times for failing to join the congratulatory herd. Facebook is not for the truth when your shit photographs* are put up. Facebook is not for the truth when you put up pictures of yourself. Facebook is not for the truth when you ask for words beginning with the letter 'S' to describe yourself. And this last example is true. The lady in question was not expecting 'syphilitic' nor had she enough humour to say she'd been cured long since. No. Opprobrium followed and it never settled. I asked myself just how needy must you be to encourage this kind of flattery. But that's Facebook. 'Tell me how much you love me.' I'll look through all my 'likes' and get a warm glow, knowing that you all think I'm as terrific as I think I am. Go and cure your syphilis I say and to hell with you.

* I recently put up a photo of myself by mistake and was embarrassed by some of the comments. No, as usual they were too kind. Didn't know I was 'gorgeous.' They should have written 'at your age

you should know better,' but they didn't. Maybe I'll make mistakes more often.

4.

After a night of heavy rain and some in the morning, it has stopped.

I'll wait till tomorrow to swing a club as the ground will be soggy.

Watched an interview with Jan Morris on YouTube. I always go to YouTube to listen to authors I'm reading. A name on a book means little but a face and a voice somehow gives the words an added resonance. If I take to you as a person, I'm more likely to take to your writing. Morris with her handsome face— (it is handsome rather than beautiful, though her history may have affected my reaction there) had particularly kind and intelligent eyes. She was seventy-four I think when interviewed and her whole demeanour spoke of a person at ease with herself and the world. I particularly noticed her eyes as you do with people. It's wholly true that the eyes mirror the soul. I've yet to see a police photograph of a criminal whose eyes didn't reflect the turmoil of a life gone wrong. Some are full of hatred, not surprising given the context of capture and conviction, while others reflect bewilderment, dull resignation or defiance. Pictures of Rose West or Ian Brady are chilling examples of how eyes reflect the soul. Have you seen Tutu's eyes?

Now there was a happy man.

As I type on my Apple keyboard I'm not alone. There is, in my keyboard, to paraphrase Robert Frost, something that does not like correct spelling. I'm going to call her Tanya Typo. The fingers get between me and my words somehow so that I'm constantly looking at the words I've made and noticing missing letters, misspellings or words attached toothers. Is this the price we pay for throwing our pens in the bin? I'm convinced that were I to write with a pen, none of this would happen, and yet here I am and will always be, looking up at the screen and seeing my constant errors till I initiate the little blue eraser to put things right. I check what I write for I hate those folk who write into newspapers commenting on articles oblivious of the errors they make. Oblivious or uncaring? Somehow for me, the message is affected by the discipline of the messenger. Don't blame him? Yes, I do. Type. Stop. Read over. Correct if necessary.

I watched the beginning of Spielberg's 'Saving Private Ryan' last night. I've seen the film before but was interested enough to watch again that opening sequence of the landings on Omaha Beach. I was blown away by the depiction of the hell that these men faced being ripped to bits by the German machine guns as they landed on that beach. Bullets zipping through water to find their targets submerged and the blood colouring the water, men drowning under the weight of their kit, others losing limbs and screaming for their mothers. The horror gets to you. Part of me horrified; another part of me wondering how they did that. Having watched footage of World War II in colour a thought struck me: I seemed more appalled by what I saw in Spielberg's film than by film of the actual landings in which I saw men mown down—real men being killed from a distance. Is this just a tribute to Spielberg's genius or does it say something about Art and Real Life? Is it just the close-ups that affect us so much? Do we sometimes fail to discriminate? Three thousand men lost their lives on that beach—by far the highest casualties of all the Normandy landings while 'only' hundreds died on the others. Evidently air power wasn't used, partly because it would have alerted the Germans to the

invasion and also it wouldn't have been ineffective

against the German bunkers.

5.

A cold bright day. Golf today with Patrick. Icy cold but clear skies, the ground, fairways and greens, hard as iron. The balls running for miles through the greens when normally they would have stopped. So gradually you adjust or try to, and hit short, prepared for the roll. Sometimes it works sometimes not. What doesn't work for me is finding my ball, looking up and staring at a tree ten yards away in direct line with the green. I hit and hope that it will shoot through the branches. Alas, the slightest touch of a branch will affect the flight of any golf ball no matter how hard it's struck.

No reading today but good air in my lungs which I'm thankful for. I lost four and two but the turning point was my tee-shot on the short thirteenth which hit the elevated green but was nowhere to be found. Gut wrenching, and psychologically crippling. Golf. Too many sevens on the card!

Watched an interview with Neil deGrasse Tyson, the personable American astrophysicist who's made a name for himself as a

populariser of things planetary. Together with Carl Sagan his books have brought understanding the cosmos within the grasp of ordinary readers. I haven't read any of these books, not because I'm not interested in things extra-terrestrial but because I find when I begin to read anything about astronomy the distances and figures generally are so beyond my grasp that it's like holding an armful of leaves. I think I have a child's understanding of the Universe: the moon isn't too far away, and you can stand on it but Mars is a long way away and you can't breathe there and there are things called 'planets' which Earth is and there are things called 'moons' and there are things called 'galaxies' and a 'black hole' is something you don't want to be sucked into. That's about it for me. It seems to me that certain subjects can only be grasped by years of dedicated study and a passion that drives this in order to begin to understand them, while others, such as that old milk stinks can be grasped very quickly. That's one 'milky' thing — Tyson's is another. What I did find interesting was his reaction to the recent flights funded by Jeff Bezos and his Blue Origin company. Passengers pay a fortune to rise sixty-five miles to the edge of Space and experience weightlessness for four minutes. My first reaction to this was that it must be nice to be so rich and play at being a spaceman. I dismissed the whole affair as a cheap publicity stunt.

When asked what he thought, Tyson said it was fine. He cited as analogy the first passenger airline flights which of course were only accessible to the rich, whereas now…Point taken. Does this mean that in a few years we'll all be jumping into a capsule for a bit of edge-of-Space weightlessness? Going to be a bit crowded up there methinks. And I'm reminded of the satellite 'junk' that is already flying about up there in orbit round our planet. How about some more? Nah. I'll just stay down here thanks. Enjoy your flight, suckers, I'm off to bed.

6.

Cold again. Beautiful sunrise at eight o'clock.

Dog not enthusiastic when offered her morning stick (an edible twist) though she took it. Not till after twelve did we discover a little pile of vomit outside a bedroom door and the stick left on the landing untouched. Poor soul wasn't feeling good.

Read more of Morris's journal. I love the honesty of it. She'll begin a page slagging off modern (English) urban youth for their phones and general attitude to life then later coming across a group of English kids in a cafe near her home in Wales, she praises their manners and their enthusiasm for life. She doesn't mind being wrong this lady. She was ninety-two when she wrote this, and it made me feel a bit

chastened. As I age, I become more and more

judgmental of the world around me: the obsession

with 'celebrity' which just seems to mean your face

has been on a TV screen: you don't need any

perceptible talent just a personality will do. The

obsession with phones and lap-tops and gaming. And

it is an obsession. Attention to these devices is all-

consuming for so many people. I pass joggers tuned

in to music who don't acknowledge the presence of

another human. I see folk in restaurants with phones

in hand, their fingers dancing, their eyes entranced,

waiting for their dishes to arrive. How about talking to

the person next to you or opposite? Oh, nothing to

say, but just noticed my friend down the road has had

sex for the first time with an alligator. Wow. Oh, that's

another hatred   — no, not the way alligators are

being sexually abused but the way the language is
being gradually eroded so that we all sound like dogs
when we're excited. I'll return to this another day: too
much mileage to rush it.

So, good on you, Jan for being open-minded at ninety
whatever. Don't think I'll make it.

7.

Dire warnings of snow on the telly. An unhealthily thin
woman on BBC Scotland sweeps her stick-like arms
over most of the country and sighs for what we are

about to face. I think past failures in predicting huge storms has forced the Weathermen and women to cover their backs by exaggerating what might be facing us. Just a wet drizzle here at noon while weather 'disruption' (they love that word) is forecast for further North. Sometimes they still get it wrong however and the recent storm, cutely named 'Arwen,' did more damage than was predicted. Sounds a bit Welsh to me but I'll refrain from any cheap racial stereotyping here and just report the after effects. I walked on the outskirts of a whole pine forest flattened on the John Muir Trail in East Lothian: trees grown in sand with shallow roots that toppled like skittles in a bowling alley before the gusts. It was Armageddon come early.

I watched an episode of the TV reality show Alaskan Bush People last night and it brought home to me again the lies that TV can proliferate. A family supposedly living a life in 'the bush' were living only a few miles from a town. The whole show was created after the patriarch of the family Billy Brown wrote a book about living in the bush. From then on, TV took over and presented the audience with lie after lie giving the folks the story they wanted to see. I've watched this with a certain fascination from the start as I'm completely captivated by depictions of people living 'in the wild.' I love to see people starving and so near to death that they begin eating themselves while listening to the low growls of a fifty-five foot grizzly bear outside their cabin. I love it when their snowmobiles run out of juice and they've got to walk back home twenty-five miles through twenty- foot snow drifts. I'm a vicarious adventurer to the distant and dangerous parts of the planet suffering for my desire to live off-grid, risking chopping off my fingers for a few sticks for my fire. I've concluded that some folk just like to suffer. Well, Billy may have lived off-grid for a time, but Brown-town is a sham. The odd thing is, that its devotees won't listen even when the truth is told: the Government didn't burn down their cabin and yes, they were taking Government hand-outs when they were not qualified to receive them. Watching their conversations with the local Alaskans I've concluded that the further you are from a city the stupider you become and language declines from words to grunts. I suppose that's how the GOP exists—America is a vast continent, and most people live very far from cities and very far from thought other than 'do we have enough wood for the fire?' or

'has that coyote got into the henhouse again?'

8.

A dusting of snow here but further south a healthy

covering. Just enough for the TV teams to remark on

stranded cars and closed roads. Our Scandinavian cousins must laugh themselves silly at how an inch of the stuff is enough to cause chaos here.

Twelfth day over, it's time to stash the baubles and the fairy lights away for another year. Our little tree is going into the garden still in its blue ceramic pot. Next year it'll be a little taller and next year I'll be a little smaller.

I love and hate Christmas. I love all the paraphernalia of celebration—the fairy lights, the carols, but even as a confirmed agnostic there's something deeply phoney about celebrating the birth of a man whose precepts most of the population have no regard for three-hundred-and sixty-five days in the year. As the years roll on it seems the clergy have given up trying to remind us of what Christmas is supposed to represent. Even the sermons denouncing materialism seem to have died out for I haven't heard any this year. That said, it's a time for the shops to make a killing, and one which can tide them over the thin months of the Winter and early Spring. We are nothing if not pragmatists when it comes to worldly things.   Omicron, Covid's last throw (we hope), has come along on the back of Delta and spooked us all into accepting more restrictions on our daily lives. Football crowds in Scotland restricted to five hundred souls which at Parkhead or Ibrox must seem like the seat cleaners have just downed tools to watch the match, whereas at East Stirling the stand will be full.

Back to Omicron and today's issue is whether Novak Djokovic will remain in his grotty hotel room in Australia while his lawyers fight to get him a visa or whether the un-jabbed star will decide enough is enough and fly from whence he came, leaving his title to someone else. Got to hand it to the Aussies though, they take no shit from big names—if you ain't jabbed you don't get in, simple as that. I read that old Djokovic (Novaxx Djocovid as some clever clog wrote in The Guardian) is a bit wacky in his beliefs. Word has it that he once stated that stagnant water could be purified by thought. He thinks molecules are amenable to emotion. Perhaps he'll meditate very hard and try to affect the molecules in Prime Minister Scott Morrison's body with his plight. Somehow, I doubt it though.

The times we live in, are, it has to be said, quite vibrant. Johnson eviscerated in Parliament by Labour's Rayner, though eviscerating Johnson isn't like eviscerating a normal person whose innards you'd see spilling —no, Johnson's innards are so hardened by eviscerating attempts they refuse to leave his body but just rise to his arms and squirm a bit before settling down again. You know he's kind of eviscerated though when the arms punch the air, his face goes red and he begins to bumble even more incoherently than usual while shaking his corn-mop. Well done, Rayner, and my, was she having a good time!

Belarus in chaos as the Prime Minister instructs the police to shoot demonstrators whom he conveniently calls 'terrorists.' Quite a useful word if you're a despot stealing all your country's oil and gas wealth to buy houses in London and being surprised when the people don't much like it. Putin of course, never far away from an opportunity, has sent in some of his stormtroopers to help his mate.

A bit of revisionism reared its head when the 'Colston Four' the main rope-pullers who tore down the statue to Edward Colston were arrested but released after trial at Bristol Crown Court. Colston, like many in the Seventeenth Century was into slavery in a big way and The Royal Africa Company was founded to extract gold and other products including slaves from West Africa. Between Sixteen-forty and Eighteen-seven it's estimated that over three million slaves were transported from Africa to The Americas. Britain grew rich from mining and slavery and men like Colston made fortunes.

I watched the mob tear down his statue and topple it into the harbour. I don't like mobs. I don't trust mobs to know what they are doing and nor does anyone else—that's why the word was invented. A mob is not a protest. A mob may assemble to protest, but a mob is a group whose individuals have lost any sense of responsibility for their actions and that's what was occurring in Bristol that day.

George Floyd's death at the hands of a cop in Minneapolis, videoed so the whole world could see it, was only one example of chronic US police violence against the black population. It led to protests against racism world-wide and Colston's topple was seen as a reasonable reaction to the exploitation of the Black Race. My problem is that this was one example of looking at history through contemporary eyes. History is full of people doing terrible things to other people—the idea that we can put these terrible things right in our present minds is absurd. If we are going to revise history to make it acceptable, then we have a job on our hands. How many other statues, buildings, Trusts, and so on, exist because of slavery or other exploitation? I believe over the years the people of Bristol have petitioned the local authority to remove the statue but without success. A 'mob' took the law into its own hands and tore it down. The statue of Winston Churchill was daubed with red paint and later sprayed with the word 'Chelsea' after Chelsea's European Cup win. Black Lives didn't matter this time—but it was another statue after all. And if it's revisionism that's your bag then why not topple old Winston. He might have saved us from the Nazis but if you read Churchill's speeches you will quickly realise that he was a racist through and through and one who believed in the superiority of the white race over any others. In addition, as a politician, he was a man whose decisions in Iraq and Bengal caused the deaths of thousands of people. Get that statue down folks and then we'll do Cecil

Rhodes. Face it—Britain wouldn't be 'Great' if it hadn't been for these men and what they did, but they were men of their time, not ours. I can see a statue to a 'meat eater' being toppled in a hundred years' time for the contribution made to Global Warming but now, today, most of us cheerfully tuck into our steaks.

I'd add to the statues of some men and women some words which explain how they made their names. Colston may be an egregious example of unfortunate stubbornness on the part of Bristol Council to at least listen to the wishes of its citizens, but the method of his removal must pose questions regarding the Law. Perhaps a vigil round the statue with each person showing Colston the red card may have worked. I've no problem with its removal—but I have a big problem with the way it was done.

'This is Edward Colston who was responsible for taking slaves from Africa to the Americas in the seventeenth Century and became very rich. Today we respect people more.' I'd maybe reduce him in size to two feet tall though, as a wee reminder that he ain't so great as he thinks he is.

The light is becoming crepuscular. Let the world sleep soon.

9.

Temperature seems as variable as moods these days. Yesterday's treacherous pavements melted during the day. Rain today and cloud which seems to have settled on The Strath.

The Colston issue rumbles on. It seems to have become Left versus Right as our Conservative Government's legal worthies to a man (and woman) have condemned the Court's decision to release the perpetrators. They are now questioning the validity of the jury's decision which seems to me to be dangerous territory. A Jury means a Jury as surely as Brexit means Brexit and you can't override the place of a jury in the judicial system just because you disagree with their verdict. We are in danger of Dictatorship in this country when our justice system is challenged by those in power. Judges have been vilified in the Right-wing press.

The Government is exercised by the issue of Judicial Reviews, seeking to challenge these when they deem politics to have intervened. As JR's can challenge Government Policy in the courts it's surely essential that these should remain untouched as a barrier to a government that could enact arbitrary laws perhaps restricting public protest unchallenged by the courts. No wonder that the Colston affair has stirred a hornet's nest among the powerful.

The Governments 'Police, Crime and Sentencing' Bill will, if it passes into law, severely restrict our power to protest with sentences of fifty-one weeks imprisonment for what would seem to be relatively minor offences such as gluing oneself to a pavement. The Extinction Rebellion movement's recent stunts blocking roads has brought storms of protest which one supposes was their objective, but it runs the risk at the same time of hardening opposition to their cause. No doubt burning letterboxes hardened opposition to the cause of the Suffragettes, but they won in the end. One can only hope that ER affect a similar conversion, though making sure granny gets back to her Care Home before lunch seems to be more important than the imminent demise of our planet in some minds.

I am learning. This morning for the second time in a few days I've restrained myself from commenting on articles in The Guardian. You know I hate it when people disagree with me. Isn't that odd? I wonder if this is a medical condition. Perhaps there's something in my brain that needs a good talking to. The trouble is we live in an increasingly divisive world and I can always predict who will disagree with me on any topic. If I wish to live at peace with myself, I've concluded, I shall avoid disagreement—particularly abusive disagreement. Luckily no one knows me. No-one knows my face. No-one who would cause me harm knows where I live and so I sleep in peace. But I don't take disagreement well. Opposing views often make me angry. I suppose I haven't the patience to try to understand where they come from, and this is because I have this solid belief that my own views are considered and fair and balanced. Consequently, if you don't agree with me you need to get a brain or develop a compassionate side. So, I no longer offer my opinion.

I used to read The Herald, a renowned Glasgow paper and commented regularly on many issues till I began to suspect that the balance of other comments was drifting in a direction away from my own convictions particularly concerning Scottish Independence. Perpetual criticism of the Scottish Government was becoming irksome, and I realised that this was probably an editorial stance. One day under the Banner of the paper I noticed the words 'A Devolutionist Newspaper.' That was the end. At least they had raised their flag.

Lunch yesterday at a nearby hotel. Very posh hotel but one I suspect is struggling. The waiter was about twelve years old. The wine we chose was delivered in an unopened bottle and placed on the table. 'What's the soup today?' We asked. 'It's tomato and red pepper.' One of my favourites. I ordered the soup. When the soup was placed in front of me it was decidedly not a red soup but a beige one. I looked up. 'It's celery soup today,' said our child waiter with no hint of explanation or apology. As I was not paying, I made no fuss, merely a shake of the head, not wishing to embarrass my host. The last time I ate here a similar experience occurred with a waiter who obviously knew nothing about the craft of waiting on a table. I wrote to the owner and was sent a voucher for £30. Interesting that yesterday's incompetent waiting was just as bad. How, I wonder can you run a hotel when your waiting staff are so incompetent? A young boy may be cheap, but he could cost you future guests.

Yes, I've e-mailed my complaint. But have had no reply. I hope the blinking place goes under. Now that's what it deserves.

10.

Absence certainly does make the heart grow fonder. A visit to Edinburgh after a two-year absence reminded me of the magnificence of The New Town. Strolling along the streets, squares and circuses with their associations with George the Third, you nudge history as your feet touch the cobbles or your eye strays down a line of 'mews' dwellings—the old coach houses. Well old George's family got their names out there—Charlotte, Frederick, Hanover and so on, though the original plan was to call Princes Street Thistle Street which George didn't like. Princes Street it was then, and the English rose got its say in Rose Street. I must say the whole thing smacks of a confidence and a vision scarcely visible in some of the modern erections many of which merely emphasise the beauty of the old. And I can't help musing on how the Union of the Parliaments in 1707 was reflected in The New Town. Three hundred-odd years ago the idea that Scotland could be so politically different from England was unthinkable but in 1707 with a ratio of five-to-one in population, England was a far richer nation and money promised to an impoverished Scotland was gladly accepted— by the rich. Today the ratio is twelve-to-one and that is the problem. The notion of 'equality' and 'mutual respect' is essential to any Union and today's imbalance in populations has made Scotland almost irrelevant in Westminster. Sixty million will always out-vote five million, as Brexit showed.

Edinburgh is a city very proud of itself. I couldn't believe the number of eating places and interesting little specialist shops to be found everywhere. I don't wonder that The Festival has contributed to this. Not only with its infusion of money (added to by The New Year jamboree) but its infusion of a cosmopolitan crowd eager for culture many of whom will return to the city at some stage.

Well, we tramped the streets of The New Town and stayed in a lovely flat in Forth Street, off Broughton Street, another reminder with its large sitting room with curved back wall of the additions to The New Town that were undertaken at the beginning of the Nineteenth Century. James Craig's original scheme was later extended North, East and West where the grandeur of the circuses

may have been a little diluted, but sufficient ambition remained to create beautiful houses.

Next door to our flat was Hart Street Studios which for twenty years produced a host of Scottish folk music including songs by The Corries.

The Downing Street affair continues and while Corn-mop (I've succumbed to name-calling to make my disgust bearable) hides behind the imminent Report by one of his lackeys, the languorous Rees Mogg puts his foot in it by calling the Scottish Conservative leader Douglas Ross 'lightweight.' His interviewer on Newsnight, Kirsty Wark, gasped. Perhaps she intuitively knew the significance of the remark. Ross, in an uncharacteristic bout of honesty and good sense, called for Corn-mop to resign and was backed by his Party in Scotland. Now, by insulting their leader one wonders where The Scottish Conservatives go. Another nail hammered into Scotland's coffin, or the first hint to Scotland's Tories that London doesn't care about them?

Went for a meal at L'Escargot Bleu, a lovely intimate French Restaurant down Broughton Street in Edinburgh. We'd been there before and I remember being particularly intrigued to see an older gent sitting at a table alone, his napkin tucked into his chin — very French. Evidently, he lunched there almost every day. And then we were given a table—his table, as it turned out. Christine sat where he had always sat, and I noticed a photo on the wall behind her. It was him, smiling shyly with a napkin hat on his head. He had died a few months ago, but his memory lived on. Good for them.

11.

Beautiful day again. Sunny and warm. Is this really the middle of January? Played nine holes but my driving was off, so I encountered a few trees.

An earthquake of 6.8 in The Pacific has caused a tsunami which has badly affected Tonga. Some feared lost.

Reading Maeve Brennan, the New Yorker columnist from the 60's and 70's. Her writing modus vivendi was sitting in restaurants and observing the human life around her. I found the first half of her book 'The Long-Winded Lady' her sobriquet in The New Yorker, rather boring. Lots of references to streets and Times Square then a few lines about a couple she'd noticed having an argument or such. Perhaps it was the chronological nature of the writing but half-way through her writing improved, and I began to see the real writer emerge. 'Real writing' for me is that moment of transcendence that occurs when description and insight take-off and another level of awareness is reached. She dislikes Sixth Avenue generally but one morning she walked it in snow and changed her mind… 'It is a perfect place for snow, and snow should always be falling there, tons and tons and tons of snow, making the avenue just about impassable, so that anybody managing to struggle through there could look at it with affection, because

Sixth Avenue possesses a quality that some people acquire, sometimes quite suddenly, which dooms it and them to be loved only at the moment when they are being looked at for the very last time.' I wonder if she ever felt guilty of neglecting her parents.

Real writing and a wonderful thought—one that as a reader makes you stop and THINK! I must say the fact that it was snow which altered her appreciation doesn't surprise me. I love snow for its magical properties and its ability to completely change a landscape or a street. Depending on the quantity, it can envelope one in a mystical way that evokes memories of childhood, of innocence, of Christmas— edges are blurred, the light is altered, softened. Snow seems to be what occurred THEN, rather than now, these Global Warming days. Last Winter here we had one dusting of snow which only lasted a day. This year, again a dusting, as if the skies lacked commitment to white. I appreciate that climate is a long- term affair and one shouldn't make assumptions, but year by year the prospect of snow recedes, which for me is a great pity.

Battling on with Animal Farm in German. Major is about to end his call to arms and in the here and now Corn-mop awaits the Report on goings-on in Downing Street. Can't believe that Sue Gray's Report will state that he broke the law, and I suspect he'll wriggle free of blame, other than that he should pay closer attention to what his staff are up to. It's astonishing to me that intelligent and reasonably honest folk in his Party can't or won't accept the moral paucity of this man. Time after time throughout his career he has been found to be lying and yet he now leads our country. Across the Pond, Trump is another liar and yet one who retains the support of better men and women in the GOP. Is Principle dead? Are there no men and women of courage and honour left to call out these rogues? Jobs-worth's rule. And If I were to be constantly called a liar I'd be pissed off. Corn-mop is used to it and it's water off a duck's back to him. Presumably if they read Ibsen, they'd all wonder what Stockmaan's problem was in 'An Enemy of the People.' 'Just keep quiet about the fucking water and life will be back to normal for you.' As to 'The Crucible' — well Proctor was a stupid prat, wasn't he? Oh, and Thomas More—well we could go on and on—just agree with the King and forget your damned conscience, Tommy Boy. Trouble is, sticking to your principles can be bad for your bank balance. Oh, God save us all from an encounter with Principle. Best not to have any really. And that leads us back to Tory-land.

Yesterday on her walk Izzy chased a hen which saved herself by lying low in a bush. The hen and some others had been wandering free of their coop and were spotted before we had a chance to put Izzy's lead on. A couple witnessed the whole affair and took such an interest in the outcome that I began to feel deeply irritated. If the dog had savaged a child, their reaction wouldn't have been different. Watched carefully, the hen was lifted free of the bush and, minus a few tail feathers returned to the coop by my partner under the watchful eyes of the walkers who if they said it once, said a thousand times, 'You'll have to report this.' I did in fact, though I doubt I would have had they not been there. Anyway, the woman at the desk just smiled and thanked me. The hen strode off to boast of how it fought the dog off and my feeling was that no-one was to blame: not my dog for doing what dogs do; not me for not expecting the hens to be out; not anyone really but The Hydro whose hens they were and who had a duty to keep them behind the wire. Looking back, I wished one of the walkers had accused me of not keeping my dog under control and I would have enjoyed a blast.

12.

Cloudy today. The threat of rain in those frowning
skies.
Izzy seems to have her stiff leg again. I'm praying it's
not arthritis. She seems to be walking ok, but after
she's rested and stands, you notice the stiffness for a
second or two.

Jan Morris again. Impressed by the references she
makes to her experiences as a reporter. Today on her
daily thousand steps she knows when it's time to turn
around when she hears the sound of the river. This
reminds her of being in Swaziland on a mountain
above Mbabane in a glade where Swazi kings were
traditionally 'scattered.' This time she was told when

she could no longer hear the stream she would be in the right place—an interesting reversal. What an amazing life this woman had. But you know when I hear the tap running and there's no-one in the kitchen, I know that it's time to turn it off. We all learn from our experiences.

13.

Another incident of mischief from Izzy. From time to time having been off the lead she refuses to return. Always in full view of whoever is with her, she stands with what we all agree is a mischievous look in her eyes and refuses to come back to the lead.

It happened last week and again today. Think a spell on the long lead may remind her of what she is missing.

A Tory defection during PM's non-answer-time to cheers from Labour, who welcomed Christian Wakeford to their ranks with his Union Jack mask on. A rare example of principle from an erstwhile rabid believer in Tory values? What happened in his head I wonder. Did he wake up this morning and realise that one Party cares more about people than the other? A damascene conversion on the road to the loo? Corn-mop interviewed yesterday seemed almost beaten but today he is rejuvenated enough to apologise with that cheeky little smile that only says one thing—some of you fuckers believe I care.

I must say, a part of me wonders what all the fuss is about. It shouldn't be a surprise that the pigs are in the farmhouse. The animals gave them an eighty-seat majority. Removing Corn-mop isn't going to change the Tory party; it will still hold the same beliefs and there will probably be the same faces round the cabinet table when the mop goes. Sunak? Truss? Gove? Oh, please not Gove. Oh, please not Truss. Oh, please not...

Putin's toy soldiers are still at the border of Ukraine in the snow.
If Ukraine and NATO refuse to be threatened by this narcissist, then his troops either slink away back where they came from, or he does the unthinkable and invades. The Ukrainians will fight like hell of course but ultimately, they will lose territory. And

68

what happens then? Guerilla tactics as Russian body bags return to Moscow? Hasn't he learned from Chechnya? No. And he is oblivious to the suffering of his people like all dictators.

We have learned what appeasement does from Munich. If you give in to the bully once he will threaten you again and again for that's what he believes works.

What we need in the face of Putin's threat is a unified response from Europe and America. At the moment the response seems to be that sanctions will be imposed on Russia, but it seems that Putin has strengthened the economy to the extent that sanctions can be borne. Days pass. The snow falls on helmets and tanks. Back to my books and the viol music.

14. Chilly day. Slight wind. Grey skies.

I'm reading Holloway's book 'Waiting for the Last Bus' the 'last bus' being death, or as common parlance has it, 'passing.' Lots of people passing these days—it's like a very busy motorway on the way to extinction or is it everlasting life? Holloway himself is quite in favour of the word 'passing' as a euphemism for dying, seeing it as a comfort to the bereaved that there just may be something else waiting for their deceased loved ones. I think he's been in the God club for too long to accept that death means extinction. Of course it's human nature to want to deny that life suddenly stops and the body decays. Love for a dead one continues, but I've never believed in an after-life. We are animals and animals die. Do mice have an after-life? 'Ah, but they don't have our brains' would be the response and my response would be 'What have brains got to do with it?' I've noticed that very clever people 'pass' just like very stupid people. Why then does Man invent an after-life for himself but not for his dog or cat or pet mouse?

When we examine some of The Church's (specifically The Roman Catholic Church) belief systems through the ages we are faced with convenient fundamental tenets such as the existence of Heaven and Hell and Purgatory. Holloway is good on Purgatory which he describes as 'a moral laundromat, where sinners who had soiled their souls on earth were slowly bleached of their stains and restored to purity.' I like that. Prayers could help elevate those whose lifts had stuck mid-way between heaven and hell however, so there was still hope for some sinners.

As a confirmed agnostic I can't read this without laughing at the stories The Church spins to keep its flocks in order. And isn't the word 'flock' interesting. Sheep ain't the brightest of creatures and not known for challenging accepted tenets. Wouldn't it be terrific if a flock of sheep got together and decided that that fucking sheepdog was for it the next time it came near them.

The Church as an institution has a lot to answer for. In the hazy days of the Middle Ages priests could extract money for a touch of The Apostle Paul's right ear or St Margaret's big toenail, as a penance for sins. What a terrific invention Sin is. Once you have established what constitutes Sin, you are flying, for you have the drop on those who believe, by dictating 'good' conduct. But being human, we need a little reward for being 'good' and that comes with a trip to Heaven. For Hindus the reward for a good life is good 'karma' in the next, which it's promised will be even more pleasant. The soul is reborn and reborn through 'samsara' the notion of 'wandering through' until it finds peace in 'nirvana.' Correspondingly, if you break the rules you go to a place the invention of which meets every horror you can imagine. James Joyce in 'A Portrait of the Artist as a Young Man' has a preacher define Hell in a parody of the fear tactics of the Roman Catholic Church. The soul will suffer in a 'Boundless extension of torment, incredible intensity of suffering, unceasing variety of torture—this is what the divine majesty, so outraged by sinners, demands…' A loving God indeed. Well, that would keep me on the right path.

Those who had witnessed the burning of heretics (those who had the effrontery to have beliefs antithetic to the accepted norm) would surely have imagined their own spell in Hell being somewhat unpleasant. Not a great future in heresy then. I'll just go with the flow. As to Muslim male martyrs and their expectation of seventy-two virgins…

It has to be said however, that Man in every culture has created belief structures which meet the human need to believe that there is some form of after-life.

Just a pity that the priests and adherents of many religions have fallen short when seen as role models of rectitude as Robert Burns celebrated in 'Holy Willies Prayer.'

For some time now the Roman Catholic Church's institutions from Orphanages (Fort Augustus Abbey School) to the Magdalen Laundries of Ireland where 'fallen women' were housed, have been exposed as places where abuses of all kinds were perpetrated by Priests and Nuns on those in their care. How can anyone cling to the belief that these institutions were beneficial in any way? Those running them, if innocent of abuses themselves, very often, it has been proved, turned a blind eye to what was occurring. Popes have apologised, but just today a recent Pope has been accused of knowing and doing nothing about abuses in Germany and elsewhere. The buck stops somewhere and it's at The Pontiff's door.

15.

A sunny day, this favoured January.

Two dogs last night. We took in a little Bedlington called Mabel, a wee grey thing with a cute face as a dry run for next week. She settled down on the sofa and slept there all night while Izzy slept on our bed upstairs. No problems of jealousy from Izzy just a bored disdain for this interloper.

Still reading Holloway on Life and Death. A few pages on the Church's concept of 'predestination.' I find the notion that our lives are mapped out for us in some way an intriguing one. Of course, 'free will' is a notion the Church cleaves to to explain man's inhumanity to man. Was there ever a debate about the existence of

God that didn't have to deal with the question of God's omnipotence? How can an all-powerful God allow children to starve in Afghanistan's snows? How can an all-powerful God allow men to engage in war and its atrocities? How can an all-powerful God desert the Jews of Auschwitz? And the answer is— He gave us 'free-will.' He gave us the choice to fuck others up. Er…why? Presumably the Church has an answer for that too. The Church has had a long time to work out its answers. Perhaps God likes a good laugh.

Our lives aren't 'mapped out' in a specific series of choices we can be expected to make, but I believe it's true that for many of us, nature and nurture are the determinants of the choices we make. We are born with a personality (and an intelligence)—some clever, some less so, some exuberant, some quiet, restrained, some adventurous— some afraid of risk. Add to this the effects of nurture and you have the package that makes you who you are. If you are loved, you are likely to be at peace with yourself and your parents will encourage you, give you the confidence to make something of your life. If you are brought up in chaos or abuse, you are likely to be ill at ease, to feel abandoned or worse, to feel no one cares about you, to be angry.

We all know how different in temperament siblings can be, and feeling loved and secure, while differences in personality may take them down different roads, in the main, they will be pleasant ones. Nurture surely is the rub—the absence of love will generally encourage poor choices that may result in a troubled life.

All of this is of course complete nonsense to the average Tory who can't quite understand why fifteen-year-old Bert from Moss Side, whose father has left home, who sleeps in the same room as his two sisters and brother, and whose mother is on the bottle, can ever become a petty thief. Class and education lead to money which leads to education and class. A quick glance at the Conservative benches in Westminster is a quick glance at 'class' in action in Britain today. Well-scrubbed and suited, they sit there—very few from homes that were less than affluent, and many such as those who form our Cabinet, extremely rich. Labour are much more colourful in their attire which befits the multifarious backgrounds from which they've emerged. To the average Conservative, Bert's misdemeanours are 'choices' he makes of his own 'free-will.' If those choices break the law, he will be put in prison—he will be punished. Rarely does compassion or understanding come into the equation. The average Tory voter doesn't do 'causes' he only does 'effects.' Bert has broken the law; therefor Bert must be punished. If we ask ourselves WHY Bert broke the law, we enter dangerous territory for the Tory because the answer to this might be that Bert has had a hard life. Bert hasn't had the sort of life we've had. Perhaps then, if we were to improve Bert's life he might not have broken the law but that might mean a compassionate welfare system and higher taxes! Interesting that the current shibboleth of the Tory programme is 'levelling up.' They certainly wouldn't contemplate 'levelling down.'

Free will. Free choices. We are all created equal. It's just that Orwell put it better. 'Some are more equal than others.' The good news for the law-abiding among us is that the Tory government are committed to providing an additional eighteen-thousand prison places by the mid-twenties. Bert and his like will be kept off our leafy streets. Tony Blair, ostensibly a socialist, but some would say an 'arch-Tory' and from an equally privileged background being a Fettes College boy, subscribed to the dictum 'Tough on crime—tough on the causes of crime.' 'Tough on the causes,' might suggest an assault on poverty, but no, that would be opening doors best left closed. Lock em up. Serves them right. Poverty is on the increase and so is crime. More prisons please.

116.

Isn't belief weird? No, I'm not mocking the beliefs of most of mankind who have faith in virgins and angels and Donald Trump and coming back to Earth as flowers or elephants or wee baby lambs having another go at living here. I know they don't like having doubts cast on their faith, and I also know that some of them get really angry so I'll just come clean and say I believe in anything that can be proved to be true. And before any Christians start to get a bit superior about the virgins let's not forget Heaven and Hell. Heaven is supposed to be some sort of 'eternal life' whatever that means, and Hell is just fucking hot—so hot that Death Valley might seem a cool place in comparison.

What exactly does 'eternal life' mean anyway? Am I still living and if so, where? Is there accommodation up there somewhere for my body or am I just left with a soul? I suppose what all this stuff comes down to is the notion of reward and punishment. If I were left to think of rewards that might tempt me in some after-life it would certainly involve sex with Kate Winslet and Susan Sarandon at least once every hour and a very nice flat overlooking a very blue and warm sea with a cook who specialised in steak au poivre. I'd need a tasty soup for lunch every day and a nice piano to play. There. I place myself at the disposal of goodness.

* Richard Dawkins in a footnote in 'The God Delusion' references Ibn Warraq who encourages would-be martyrs to avail themselves of seventy-two virgins on Earth rather than give up the ghost to munch on 'white raisins of crystal clarity' in Heaven. 'Huris' refers to food, not girls, evidently.

17.

Sky the colour of slate but from somewhere sunlight on the next-door wall.

Reading the Guardian and an article suggesting that Corn-mop and his government, have surely jeopardised any remaining faith the British electorate have in their politicians. Not a view with which one could disagree, but you wonder what has really changed. Politicians in the Tory Party have always come from a certain stratum of society rather above the norm in wealth and other privileges. Britain is a class-ridden society and has been for a very long time: 100% of Anthony Eden's Government in 1955 went to fee-paying schools. In 1979, 91% of Margaret Thatcher's cabinet went to fee-paying schools. Tony Blair's Labour Cabinet in 1997 saw a reduction to 32%—hardly a towering endorsement of Labour's support for 'the workers.' Now Johnson's lot are up to 60%. Fee-paying schools mean wealth. It costs £48,000 a year to send your child to Eton—almost double the average salary.

 The question arises then, is this unique to Britain, this issue of a rich ruling elite?

It's often thought that other European countries don't have private schools, but this is not so. Only Finland has a policy of state education banning private schools charging fees, though there are a few 'faith schools' outside the state system. In other countries 'faith schools' exist similarly vis- -vis the system but must generally adhere to a strict line in the charging of fees. In France, 20% of pupils attend fee-paying 'lyc es' though the fees are relatively low which mitigates against the exclusive nature of these institutions, enabling even parents with modest incomes to access them for their children should the latter pass the entrance qualifications. Germany also has some private schools but like France the fees are modest. It does seem that Britain is on its own in discriminating between the 'have's' and 'have-not's' when it comes to education with the concomitant social privileges attached to the 'public school' system ensuring the continuance of a class-ridden society. I live within two-hundred yards of a fee-paying school and as I see the scrubbed bright faces of the boys and girls passing (the girls in their kilts) I can't help but think that their paths through life are going to be much easier than most of the pupils attending the local Academy. Here are the lawyers and accountants and the engineers and the doctors of the next generation just as their parents were those of the previous one. Just as the marque of your car or your address labels your success, so does the school your child attends in this small town.

Class and tradition are two aspects of British political life that seem to be so intrinsic that no Government is willing to examine the effects of them on our political health. The very Houses of Parliament itself, (barring the odd fire or two) built in 1512, still houses our Houses of Commons and Lords, chambers from another age, the former too small to seat every MP and with no modern electronics to facilitate voting but the age-old system of filing through 'Aye' or 'No' lobbies for a Division Vote. Tradition rules OK. And tradition can be the enemy of change or progress. Our First Past the Post system of electing MP's pays no heed to the overall number of voters in the country supporting a particular Party, so that a Tory majority in Parliament can exist when the number of votes cast nationally may have been greater for another Party. Our adversarial system leads to a two-party chamber in which the Government benches support the Government, and the Opposition benches oppose the Government because that's their raison d'etre— to oppose. Most countries in Europe use some form of

Proportional Representation to decide their Parliaments. Only Britain and France use FPTP but in France an elected candidate must gain more than half the votes cast to be elected.

One wonders what it would take for Britain to decide that the system of 'in-power' and 'not-in-power' in a Parliamentary chamber is a system destined to foment factionalism at the expense of decisions that might no longer be dependent on dogma but on good sense. Why shouldn't the best minds of whatever Party be those who come together to make the best decisions? Will a Labour Party under Keir Starmer if elected in 2024 change the voting system to PR? I doubt it. And so, tradition with its gaiters and black rods and uncomfortable green benches; with its little 'neutral' Queen reading out her government's proposals will continue to prevail over new ideas and new directions while Britain sinks into a bog of political archaism. Britannia may once have 'ruled the waves' but she has sprung a leak and is sinking fast under a captain scanning the horizon for a mythical sunny upland.

18.

Cloudy.

I read a poem on Facebook this morning
celebrating Burns Day. A chap playing his bagpipes
somewhere (England?) as if bagpipes were
representative of Burns. Facebook. I've said before
and I'll say again—what is the point exactly? (not of
Burns—I can see the point of him) and I can see the
point of raising money for a good cause, and I can
see the point of telling all the neighbours that your
cat has gone missing and putting up a picture of
pussy and I can see the point of advertising

interesting artistic events and I can see the point of other less personal things but when it comes to the personal I don't see the point, apart from seeking praise or in some cases, money. Who cares that your grandfather if he'd lived would have been two hundred years old yesterday or that this is the wonderful pizza you ate last night at Mario's? And who cares that this is a photo of you when you were sixteen? Who cares that you've taken a boring photo of a sunset? Who cares if you've just self-published your fortieth novel? And what do you want when you put up a poem about Burns? If some folk like it, they'll tell you how terrific it is or more probably if they 'kind of' like it they'll give you a wee 'like' out of loyalty. But what of the folk that don't think it's up to much? Ah, there's the rub. Is there room for them to criticise your poem? You hope not—that's not part of the deal, is it? Here's my poem about Burns that I'm terrifically proud of and you'd better be too, for if you demur, you'll not only upset me but those of my 'friends' who posted a 'like.'

I must come clean here and admit that I've posted a poem myself and got forty-seven 'likes.' Poacher turned gamekeeper. But you know, I knew it wasn't a great poem and didn't deserve so much attention though it was germane to the moment. I won't post another though as I don't see the point. Seeking praise says something about you that doesn't quite sit well with me— must be my Scottish Calvinist stock.

Reading Seamus Heaney again, I love the overt sensuality of his poetry. He is a master at depicting the senses: in 'Bogland' the earth is 'black butter', in 'Undine' the water 'rippled and churned' in the drainage ditch. I almost touched the hem of his greatness once on a bridge in Cambridge as I passed him in conversation with someone. Great man, I believe, and a great poet.

Another winter's day that has forgotten it's winter. No sun, but warmer than it should be. Rain tomorrow is forecast.

The Ukraine issue smolders on. America has 8,500 men on stand-by ready to bolster the NATO states bordering Russia. I've no faith in a narcissist like Putin being able to admit he's made a strategic blunder in all this. I expect an invasion. Sweden and Finland may join NATO. Well done, Vladimir.

18.

Another sunshiny day.

I'm dipping into Montaigne's Essays as tentatively as you dip into a steaming bath. Like the bath, you must be patient and brave it till you feel comfortable with the temperature. With the essays, you need to adjust to their time of writing and look for the timeless gems. Interesting that the word 'assay' is the origin of 'essay.' An attempt, an apprentice effort meant to be an assessment of skill. As we 'assay' silver to determine its purity the apprentice piece is judged for the skill of its maker.

For a man of the Sixteenth Century the subjects of many of his essays still exercise our minds today: 'On Educating Children,' 'On Solitude,' 'On Drunkenness', 'On the Length of Life.' He has some interesting things to say about dying: 'What madness it is to expect to die of that failing of our powers brought on by extreme old age and to make that the target for our life to reach, when it is the least usual, the rarest kind of death.' Not sure about 'the target' bit—I'd imagine that would be quite a reasonable target, to die naturally rather than in war or by an accident, but we must remember the age he lived in—an age in which medical practices didn't extend much beyond giving leeches a good meal or shoving a dirty rag in the patient's mouth as his leg was amputated. In an age of wars, and looking back, it seems, continual strife, such words make good sense, but you've got to wonder if what he is really saying is Don't expect to die of natural causes folks—you'll probably be eviscerated by an enemy sword or immolated in your village by a foe before old age takes you. Not much consolation, but very true in a 16th Century France riven by civil wars. Of what relevance then, might Montaigne's words have in today's world?

The life span of someone living in Britain today is in the region of 75-85 years, women living longer than men (blame testosterone and size, gentlemen) while in France in the 16th century it was 40 years. Montaigne himself had enough money to retire to his estate and write and died at 59 of 'quinsy,' a disease of the tonsils which deprived him of speech, one of God's little jokes that would have been funny on a man who loved to talk, but on one who loved solitude not a big deal. But his pragmatic take on death resonates today when we live in an age which seems to fear death in a way our ancestors didn't. The 'madness' of expecting to die naturally has in our society become so established that dying itself is seen as something to be fought. Yes, religion plays a strong part in easing the idea with its belief in 'everlasting life' but when you take away spiritual cushions what are you left with? In an increasingly un-spiritual or material age where science seems to have successfully challenged Montaigne's dictum that we shouldn't hope, or even expect to die 'naturally', medical advances have provided us with the means to extend our lives in many cases beyond our faculties. As Richard Holloway puts it, 'the narcissism' of the modern age 'supplies the energy for one of the main enterprises of modern capitalism, the Anti-Ageing and Postponement of Death industry…we spend fortunes delaying death and the physical dissolution that precedes it.' He goes on to assert that we try to escape 'the anguish of death' always believing it has come for us too soon.

He's right of course, and the result of medical advances means that we can keep people alive when their 'quality of life' is very poor. I wonder if there will be a proliferation of 'care homes' in the future with the concomitant drain on our care services and NHS. While life-expectancy figures have risen during the Twentieth Century, they do not tell the whole story. Men in England may live to 79 years and women to 83, but their 'healthy lives' are much shorter. Statistics show that men will be healthy till they are in their early sixties but may then face sixteen years of poor health as will women.

Keep taking the pills folks. Though Montaigne may have seen the 'rarest kind of death' meaning old age, as a blessing in 17th Century France, today old age comes with a Russian Roulette of ailments that some may regard as far from a blessing.

19.

In these troubled times for Downing Street, it's interesting to see which faces are permitted to pop up to prop up the Government. The elongation that is Rees-Mogg of that ilk, a man rarely exposed to televisual glare, has appeared on Newsnight more than once in the last few weeks, his rubbishing of Douglas Ross as 'lightweight' not enough to throw a cloak over his head and banish him to whatever fastness is his residence. No, he's back, and old Kirsty, whose wardrobe has turned mournfully black of late, is doing the needful. His latest comment on recalcitrant Tories was to suggest that if the Dear Leader falls on his rubber sword it may be time to call a General Election. Now, if this wasn't a grenade thrown at the Tory doubters, I don't know what would be. An election now, when Labour are a few points ahead in the polls might just be the end for those Tories sitting in marginal seats. Do I hear the sound of squeaky bottoms? So, the choice would be clear—

support Johnson or lose your seat. Well now, that's a tricky one isn't it…

An article in The Guardian today by Polly Toynbee focusing on wee Rishi Sunak as a possible successor to Johnson. She details Rishi's rise from Winchester, through Oxford (PPE) then a Fulbright to Stanford (MBA) and a job with Goldman Sachs. He was something to do with money for hedges there and presumably while he was buying them or cutting them, he met a woman who was a billionaire and married her. Presumably because he loved her. Toynbee's take on wee Rishi is that he hasn't got the balls to show just how much he wants to be PM, sitting there as Chancellor, his hands under his bum while lisping Liz Truss parades through the media telling us all what a gift Johnson is. Now Liz has just got herself into a bit of difficulty by flying somewhere in the Government plane at an estimated cost of £500,000 while vast swathes of the working population are taking home another tin of Heinz Beans from the local food bank for their starving kids. It seems the best thing Tories can do is to remain in bed with their duvets over their heads until The Gray Report concludes that Johnson's happy-go-lucky style of government while not perfect, cannot be said to be law-breaking. Johnson himself is now under attack, accused of 'authorising' the transport of a plane load of dogs from Afghanistan while Afghani interpreters working for the British government were left standing on the tarmac at the tender mercy of the Taliban. Of course, he denies it, but then he denies everything. I've now learned that if you deny everything then you're probably guilty of everything.

There's probably a psychological thing at play here. He called this accusation 'rhubarb.' Perhaps that's what Eton boys call anything they don't like. Maybe in one of his less guarded moments he might even call the present state of things a 'mess.'

My ruminations on death yesterday were brought up short with the news that my children's stepfather fell down dead of a heart attack on his way to doing my daughter's garden. I'd never met him, but I felt deeply for my ex-wife in her trouble.

My brother remarked that at our time of life there is rarely good news such as a birth or any joy. How true. It seems we are all on a downhill slope and though there is no cure for advancing years there is help for ageing brains and failing hopes. Doing something NEW is always an option and will slow the pace of decline. As I look through my window, I notice the first blossoms on the cherry tree in the next-door garden. Housman's 'fifty Springs' may have felt there was 'little room' for him to enjoy its 'snow,' but for me I'll enjoy it while I can and cursed be he that asks, 'how old are you?'

20.

For as long as I've allowed myself to think about my own funeral, I've taken the line that I don't want all that crematorium 'fuss': the black ties and dresses, the grim faces, the minister that never knew me and probably the usual dreary hymns. There is an inverted self-regard at play here of course—I think of myself as different, maybe more critical of 'the run of the mill.' For most of us who regard ourselves as introverts, who avoid the fuss of life's celebrations, who prefer to listen rather than talk, to watch rather than participate, the thought of a eulogy by a stranger is one of life's rituals to be avoided. No, I won't be there to raise the coffin lid and shout out 'get on with it!' but oddly, irrationally, my leaving matters in an 'it doesn't matter' sort of way. So, my casual response to 'what would you like' was always—a plain box and maybe a happy tune. Who cares? I won't be there. It was my brother who changed my view. A good friend of his, a lecturer, indicated in the strongest terms to his wife and family that he didn't want any of the usual trappings. His last few months were spent in pain and there may have been an anger lingering in him against his own demise. In any event, my brother insisted on attending and he told me it was the sorriest event he'd ever attended. It must have felt like being the only diner in a restaurant. Only two or three family and no other mourners. It felt as if the man had excluded the many who'd miss him. It wasn't a fitting departure my brother thought, for a man of such accomplishment and it made him feel bad. He thought the family had been cheated in some way.

When I heard his account, I understood better that a funeral is not only about the deceased but about those left behind: that my previous stance had been selfish. Richard Holloway puts it well when he writes of a man who 'couldn't be bothered to turn up at his own funeral' by refusing any eulogy. The point being made is that echoed by my brother, that a funeral is as much about the grieving as the deceased, and if you deny the grieving their rights, you deny them the healing process.

Let there be colour then, let there be music and birds and trees. Oh, and let me lie in a cardboard box for that would please my partner. Not that she wants me dead, but she believes in cardboard over wood! I'm still thinking about the songs but mainly I want everyone to be happy.

I've thought. I want 'The Norland Wind.'

And speaking of winds: strong winds today. Storm Malik. The names may change but the effects are the same—some deaths, pictures of roofs blown off and huge trees landing on cars. Tomorrow a new one is coming. I'd call this 'thick and fast'.

21.

As Covid rumbles on like a storm moving away and growing fainter, for some (the many unvaccinated) the thunder is still very present. On T.V. last night, a patient suffering from Omicron, an Indian gentleman with a beard, lay intubated (how our vocabulary expands in a crisis) and we saw the tube gently extracted from his throat. He took his first painless breath. He was asked why he hadn't been vaccinated and said, 'fear of the unknown, I suppose.'

Fear of the unknown may be a human instinct, but the unknown is really 'la condition humaine.' None of us know with much certainty from one minute to the other what lies in store for us. Thankfully. If we did, one can't imagine what our daily lives would be like. If we broaden the 'unknown' beyond knowing that the kettle will boil, life can be scary. If we imagined that 'the unknown' might be death, severe discomfort or mental annihilation how would we cope? Yes, of course there is a problem. If you knew that driving your car to work was going to result in your death, you wouldn't drive to work, you'd probably go back to bed and that would be a good choice. But the next day you might drive to work and die. Got you. Didn't say which day. There is no future for mankind in 'fear of the unknown.' Columbus certainly wouldn't have reached the Indies had he feared the unknown, as his crew did, but on the other hand Hitler wouldn't have invaded Russia had he feared the unknown or knew anything about Napoleon's 'Grande Armee' and we'd all be speaking German today. Conclusion: fear of the unknown can affect your conduct to your advantage but also to your disadvantage.

Of course, it's always possible in certain contexts to predict what is going to happen. When our Indian gentleman was struggling to breathe it was possible to predict that a tube would be inserted into his trachea and 'breathing' would occur without pain. It was not by chance that our gentleman was Indian. There seems to be a cultural issue at play which encourages certain ethnicities to distrust vaccination more than others. The issue of misinformation is another which mitigates against take-up of the vaccine, and it was interesting to read that two musicians have now withdrawn permission to play their music on the streaming service Spotify because it affords airtime to the anti-vaccine propagandist Joe Rogan under the flag of 'free speech.' There is a high percentage of non-vaccinated people in London of course, and a city of this size embraces many ethnicities. What can be said according to the data is that people who are not vaccinated or 'boosted' are as much as eight times more likely to find themselves in hospital than those who are fully vaccinated. Were we not vaccinated against polio, T.B., smallpox, flu, measles, and a host of other potential diseases one wonders how we would fare.

Not a covid storm but another one coming later today. Corrie. Just don't kill my cordyline.

22.

Storm over. A blustery night with little sleep. All calm this morning. Cordyline still standing proud.

Reading Montaigne, I came across a comment allegedly made by Socrates in response to being told that a man had not been improved by travel: 'I am sure he was not,' Socrates said, 'he went with himself.' Note, not 'by himself' which would have been a tad commonplace for the Socratic brain, but 'with himself.' The meaning is clear: travel broadens the mind that is open to be broadened.

Having travelled a little but continually meeting those who have travelled a lot, I've often wondered just how broad their minds must be compared to mine.

Looking back, I accept that I travelled 'with myself' suspicious of people and customs that were strange to me.

To 'travel' in the accepted sense, rather than merely moving from your town to the next on the top of a bus, or spending two weeks in Benidorm eating Full English Breakfasts, suggests experiencing and acknowledging a different culture (or preferably multiple cultures). Dress, food, architecture, language, religion and many other differences all contribute to the challenges of travel, and Socrates is surely right when he asserts that the traveler's ability or willingness to open himself to be altered in some way by his experiences is crucial to the benefit it will bring.

I have spent time in France, Germany, Spain, Portugal, Italy and the USA but the furthest I have travelled out of Europe and the greatest cultural shock I experienced was to spend two weeks in Guatemala in Central America. We rented a modern villa half-way up a jungled hillside overlooking Lake Atitlan. Between us and the lake was the village of Jaibalito, a small collection of breeze block 'huts' between the avocado trees. The only way into the village is by boat for there are no roads round the lake.

What strikes the European when he exits his comfortable existence in the industrialised West, is the realisation that what he has, and accepts as the norm, is denied millions in the rest of the world whose norm is to earn enough to eat. The average Guatemalan subsists on a diet of corn tortillas, beans and some vegetables. The varied Western diet is beyond the means of most of the population.

It is a country rife with corruption in which 60% of the land is owned by 1% of the population. So, what mind-expanding was done during my stay here?

Firstly, I experienced poverty, real poverty—not British 'poverty' which is defined by the proportion of your income spent on heating or other aspects of living—but a poverty of hope. Secondly, I realised that poverty such as that experienced by these villagers does not adversely affect an indomitable spirit, a cheerful resolve to make the best of what life offers, whether it be a job stoking up our hot tub (I know, I know, the very sound of it makes me cringe) or cleaning the houses of the few ex-pats who live near the village. There is no clearer light to be shone on poverty than that which illuminates the disparity between master and servant—between he who can pay and he who needs pay. The Americans, Irish and Norwegian folk who have decided to live there, are to an extent living 'the life of Riley' with low prices and no taxes. The few quetzals they pay the locals for services are nothing to them, yet there is no resentment that I detected. There is a resignation that probably contributes to the 'contentment' of these people with their lot.

I watched in awe the first day as a small man (they are all small--malnutrition?) heaved our two heavy cases on his back and carried them up the hundred steps to our villa. I was reminded of seeing sherpas on Everest carry enormous loads that would kill the Westerner. But to this little man it was worth the effort. And of course, we were advised how much to pay him. Mustn't spoil them.

Near the end of our stay a fire broke out in the forest above us driven by strong winds. We fled the house with our cases (yours truly in the vanguard!), helped of course by the villagers as some made their way past us to fight the blaze. I was terrified, imagining the whole village scrambling into the sea to avoid immolation, and watched from the roof of a village house as the blaze was fought up the hillside. Our villa was spared owing to their efforts, but the woodpile nearby burned like a bonfire.

One enduring issue struck me: when visiting a country where the population are poor, as a traveler you must be conscious that you will be seen as a rich man and a customer for what they can offer in exchange for money. I often felt that they were using me, that I was being cheated. And they were using me as a purchaser of their goods in many instances, whether a pair of brightly coloured Guatemalan trousers or a brightly painted picture of a woman with a basket of fruit on her head. Only once did I feel cheated however, when the owner of a boat we were on refused to land until we had given him what an American on board (a resident) assured us was an extravagant fare.

My travelling companions were all female and were much less suspicious of being 'rooked' than I was, but I learned that you must trust people. I also learned that you are engaging in a kind of social contract by buying things you may not really need. How many wall hangings do you need? How many scarves or shirts do you really need? You buy them and in doing so you help in a small way to alleviate the struggles of these people.

There is then a vast difference between travelling to such a country as Guatemala and travelling in Western Europe. Travelers or foreigners everywhere are a target for the unscrupulous and the down-right wicked but in Guatemala with one exception we were met with kindness and honesty. In Spain, my partner left her glasses in a taxi and when we traced the driver, he refused to return them unless we paid for a day's tour of Barcelona. Now that's not friendly or honest. We declined.

As I've admitted, my female companions' minds were more open than mine on this trip to Guatemala but If I set out with little but myself, I'm certain I came back with a much-expanded view of the world and the diversity of its inhabitants. I learned that poverty does not necessarily lessen the spirit and that 'travel', real travel, does not involve 'seeing the sights' but understanding and accepting the conditions in which people live who live different lives.

We now sponsor a Guatemalan girl whose family circumstances have been immeasurably improved by our regular donations—donations which negligibly affect our circumstances.

At the moment I'm reading the travels of a writer who epitomises a willingness to immerse himself in other cultures. I'll return to Ryszard Kapuscinsky later in this journal.

23.

Grey skies with little islets of blue.

Signing up.

As I watch television footage of white-camouflaged soldiers preparing for war on the Ukrainian border, I can't help wondering what is in the mind of the recruit who signs himself up for the army of whatever nation. You don't have the privilege of dictating the terms under which you will fight; you may be called on to fight to save your country from an invader, or as must be the case if you are a Russian soldier at this moment, you must accept the role of invader. What does Ivan think as he drives his tank hither and thither in the snow at the whim of Vladimir Putin? Is he fully up with the political manoeuvres of The Kremlin and supportive of the conviction that invading Ukraine is vital to stop the incursions of NATO in Western Europe? Or is he just a soldier who signed up to leave everything behind but obedience to his commander? Does Ivan realise that he is quite likely to be fried in his tank or does he think it will be someone else that dies? We've been waging war for thousands of years and soldiers have died in many cases for no gain to their countries. Is life so little to be cherished?

My problem is I like being alive, that's why If I were Ivan, I'd rather sleep on a bench in Izmaylovsky park wrapped in The Moscow Times than be preparing to give my life for the expansionist dreams of an ex-KGB Intelligence Officer whose government clings to power by controlling 60% of all newspapers and all TV channels. I lie at night imagining the first guns roaring and I dread what will ensue. If Ivan had sense, he'd get all his chums together and they'd say, 'fuck this for a game of soldiers, we're off home.' Of course, they can't—they signed up and they must pay the price, much like politicians do.

Ah, politicians. Now there's another bag of tricks. And it's not a million miles of a leap to link the ambitions of one man in Russia to the flourishing narcissism of 'Corn-mop' here. Boris Johnson's shenanigans in Downing Street where parties took place during strict 'lock-down' for the rest of Britain, has forced him into denials and obfuscations the like of which the Commons has never witnessed in living memory. 'Wait till the Gray Report is published' is the default setting to any direct questioning of his presence at the 'parties.' Rarely if ever has such evasion been so blatant. And rarely if ever has such a tactic been so infectious among party adherents. Like soldiers, all politicians sign up to a creed—to obey the Party Line. Now no-one will be summarily shot if he demurs from this line, but he is likely to lose his seat and his/her pleasant lifestyle when next the electorate puts pen to paper. In normal times (those we remember when politicians 'seemed' to possess integrity) it was possible to show disagreement within the bounds of what is conveniently termed 'the broad church' of any Party. The lash of the Whips was enough to keep you in line. But we live in different times when a Prime Minister who flagrantly and obviously has engaged in conduct unbecoming his Office is being supported by his troops in the face of Truth, Integrity, Justice, and any other moral notion available.

The Conservative party knew what this man was like from his past exploits in journalism where his columns, thinly veiled as humour, exhibited bigotry and racism. Yet they elected him their leader because he had outward charm enough to fool the electorate into thinking him worthy of office. He was a card. He 'got Brexit done' and he promised to 'level up'— a man who crosses the stream of truth by the slippery stepping- stones of slogan. Now 'I get it—I'll fix it' is the latest stone in his crossing. There aren't many stones left for him to step on before he slips and tumbles headfirst into the water, but as he crosses his supporters are applauding his efforts from the bank.

Some people are unequipped through plain stupidity or ignorance to see the truth of what stares them in the face and some are equipped but will not admit what stares them in the face. The GOP is not a party of fools, yet they supported a man so obviously flawed as Donald Trump. If one asks why, there is no other answer than that it was to their benefit. If you question your leader, you lose. You lose your seat, and you lose the chance to ever be elected again. So, the Johnsons and the Trumps of this world continue on their dubious ways and we edge closer to the death of democracy. When individuals who represent us no longer recognise integrity or principle what hope do we have?

Boris Johnson and Truth are not strangers—they are enemies, and yet he still wins the support of the majority of his party. Are these people also devoid of any virtue? Some eminent Tory voices have spoken out, but they are few among the nodding donkeys that bray in The House. When you became an MP, your commitment was not only to your Party but your country. When your country is in peril because of your Party, then do your duty and resign your post. Go with your conscience clear, your principles intact. Ivan can't leave his tank for he knows he'd be shot, but losing your job as an MP is not losing your life. When we no longer trust our leaders what is left for us? As Robert Bolt had Thomas More say in his play 'A Man for all Seasons:' "This country is planted thick with laws, from coast to coast, Man's laws, not God's! And if you cut them down, and you're just the man to do it, do you really think you could stand upright in the winds that would blow then?" For the craven Richard Rich, the object of that swipe, swap Boris Johnston.

The Tory Party have a leader that believes Law is for others, not him. May he topple in the winds that blow and may he take with him the lickspittle cowards that cheer him on.

24.

A calm day. Sunshine on the cherry tree.

Thoughts today on the irascible Ian Blackford.

Ian Blackford the leader of the SNP group was

ejected from The House of Commons a few days ago

for calling Boris Johnson a liar. True perhaps, but a

breach of Parliamentary etiquette as I'm sure

Blackford knew. Now Blackford is an angry wasp in

the hair of Corn-mop and one he is constantly batting

away. Tory disdain for Blackford, it isn't too much of

an exaggeration to say, is symptomatic of their disdain for the party he represents, for The Scottish National Party have all but destroyed the Tory Party in Scotland (both the British Conservative Party and the Scottish one, though the latter survive in a parliament which runs on a hybrid of P.R. and F.P.T.P.) In recent years successive Tory governments have been elected by the overwhelming numerical superiority of voters in England, and this has virtually disenfranchised Scottish voters who feel they are being run by political aliens in Westminster. Margaret Thatcher's decision to use Scotland as a guinea pig for her 'poll tax' in 1989 and the next year in England, led to riots. That Dukes and dustmen might pay the same charge saw the essential flaw in the system. Scotland never forgave the Conservative Party for its imposition of The Community Charge as it was called—designed to attack Labour overspending councils, and since then the Scottish National Party have flourished as the flagbearers for what many Scots see as the only way to rid themselves of Tory rule—independence. The Scottish 'National' Party is a title of some significance seeing a fully independent Scotland making her own way in the world as a nation state. But is 'nationalism' the future or is it the past? And where does it lie with Patriotism?

George Orwell wrote that Nationalism was '...to identify oneself with a single nation or other unit, placing it beyond good and evil and recognising no other duty than that of advancing its interests.' If we dwell for a moment on 'placing it beyond good or evil' we may acknowledge the more blue-tinted adherents of Scottish Nationalism—the Saltire-waving marches, the bagpipes, the drums, folk draped in flags and even, it must be said, an Anti-English sentiment among some. Tick. But the 'no other duty' part seems a little strong in today's world.

Orwell went to Spain in 1936 to fight against Franco's nationalists. Orwell's Europe was perhaps even more volatile than today's -a world in which German Nationalist sentiment was on the rise and the clouds of war hung heavily over every head. Since then, Nationalism as the flag-waving boundary-expanding aim of every nation has been ameliorated by those calm European heads that brought the European Union into being. The Baltic states of Latvia, Lithuania and Estonia became independent nations after the collapse of The Soviet Union and continue to thrive. We might question whether their 'nationalism' is a threat to their neighbours but it's unquestionably true that the size of a nation encourages the belief that its 'interests' may widen at the expense of the interests of its smaller neighbours. Germany and Russia are both states whose sense of 'national interest' have adversely affected the integrity of their neighbours. While Orwell's definition of, and dislike of 'nationalism' may in some cases be justified, he does not condemn feelings which men may have for their countries.

He defines 'Patriotism' as the obverse of 'Nationalism,' namely, 'devotion to a particular place and a particular way of life which one believes to be the best in the world but has no wish to force on other people.' In essence, Patriotism good—Nationalism bad. The patriot feels good about himself and his country—the nationalist thinks everyone should be like him and might just try to bring that into being.

The Scottish National Party, in spite of the name, are very aware of the disdain attaching to Orwell's narrow-minded, dangerous Nationalism and take pains to assert their international aims. They are 'patriots' under a Nationalist umbrella, seeking good relations with other countries and wishing to rejoin the club which English voters forced them to leave. English 'Nationalism' which forged the British Empire and the arrogance of which has chosen to place Englishness above Europeanness is a different beast. Regaining power over your own people when you were once a Nation which through the greed of a rich few relinquished its sovereignty, is I believe an aim that few could oppose. We are patriots here in Scotland and I'm sure George would approve. We are at heart a generous crowd. Why even a Scottish

whirlpool spared our George.

25.

Someone made the point that growing old increasingly puts you in the position of an alien suddenly appearing on Earth. As you turn around you can't help thinking 'this is all weird stuff.' As you mature with experience, little by little modernity begins to assail you, in many cases ushering your accepted beliefs out the door. As time passes, much of what you believed and that made you 'You' has gone like dandelion seeds blown by the winds of change. It's not just a case of 'Oh, keep up', that phrase that knives you when it's directed at you by someone of a different generation; when the references are lost, so are you. When you're no longer a part of the zeitgeist you might as well be dead. When Popular Culture, Social Media, and social mores undermine all you have been comfortable with, you either shrivel into nothing or respond. Learning that your 'comfort' was someone else's pain, can come as a shock.

The habit of looking back has two faces: one is the effect of nostalgia, which can seem like edging into a warm bath; the other the chill of 'now' over 'then.' Why is our instinct when looking at a photograph of ourselves fifty years before, to mock our hairstyle or our dress? 'Look at those trousers!' we exclaim at the bell-bottoms of the sixties, 'How could I have worn them!' Flower power—what was all that about! Well, you wore them just the same as you wear your clothes today— it's called fashion, and it changes. But while fashion changes and our tastes with it, other changes are not so easily made; attitudes are not like trousers, they can't be replaced so easily.

I grew up in the sixties when homosexuality was a crime. Not until the Wolfenden Report recommendations were made law in England in 1967 was homosexual relations between consenting adults over 21 legalised. In Scotland it took till 1980 and in Northern Ireland 1981.

In 1967 I was twenty-two years old. Is it a wonder my father warned me to watch out for 'poofs' when I went to London aged seventeen? He even suggested I have buttons on my flies rather than a zip, in case the latter failed and presumably my member would pop out for a breath of air. I didn't walk round London with my hands guarding my crotch, but his words were still in my head somewhere.

I'm not sure how change comes about, but my learned homophobia has withered through time and exposure to homosexual men and women portrayed in the media. And quite right too. I suppose as I matured, I learned that in every society through the ages there have been homosexual men and women and that it's no-one's right to deny another his/her natural instincts. 'Different strokes for different folks' was a good lesson and one age makes more poignant.

T.V. is perhaps the most effective driver of social change through exposure to alternative views and ways of living. Naturally the Theatre and Literature both play a part, but those exposed to these art forms are in the minority while nearly every home has a television. The acceptance of 'diversity' has come a long way during my lifetime, and it has affected the way I think without my having actively sought to change any of my prejudices. Now I'm 'getting on', my remaining prejudices such as they are, are not taken seriously.

In company I avoid airing some of my hang-ups for there would be no audience. If I were to explain my feelings about how the mobile phone has a generation or two in its thrall, I would be laughed at. Who wants to know that they're addicted to something? Yes, I have one—how can you exist without it now? Who wants me to explain that talking to a face on a screen is less interesting than talking to a real face whether in a lecture hall or a doctor's surgery? Who wants me to suggest that the more the media talk about young people's mental health, the more young people will begin to question their mental health? It's as if 'mental-health' has just been invented as another issue that young people have to deal with in this world of 'issues.' And this leads me to the burden of my long-winded song— who invented 'the trigger warning?'

I only became aware of this in literature as I was studying for an

MLitt degree. There at the top of many pieces submitted for reading in the workshops by students much younger than me would be the words 'trigger warning' and the writer would explain the dangers of reading it or listening to it.

I'd always thought triggers were something that John Wayne would finger, but no, they were set right here. Read this and you'll trigger something you'll regret; a warning to the reader that he/she might be shocked by what they read. Well, to be honest, I was often shocked in the 'workshops', but more by the puerility of the writing than by any references to violence, sado-masochism or sexual activity. But then, I'd been warned, so that was fine. If the word 'blood' was to appear, I could leave, before I vomited all over the lovely young girl next to me. Of course, platforms such as Netflix and Amazon Prime have been using such warnings for some time. Not classified as 'triggers' as such, I always regarded them as some sort of summary of the content. In fact, when I'm warned of nudity, sexual this or that and a bit of violence I'm all for it. They should call them 'enticements.' Where then did 'triggers' originate? And why do we now have a generation of folk who are offended so readily?

In an age of 'diversity' it seems the diversity extends to the many aspects of our lives that pain each of us in some way. In American Colleges warnings started to appear in the early 2000's particularly when issues of feminism and male violence against women were being discussed. It was thought appropriate to warn members of the audience that some of the views or accounts given might trigger a Post Traumatic Response to similar events in their own lives. While there may have been some genuine concern at that time over that issue, the practice spread to encompass any controversial issue that was under debate. You've been warned, so what do you do? Go somewhere else for a cup of tea? Or do you sit it out and learn? Many professors in Colleges across America it's argued, now seek to avoid controversial issues which may give offence. As always, the habit has spread to Britain. When America is offended you bet, we can be too.

Edinburgh, The LSE, Oxford, Goldsmith's and Stirling among other institutions have employed 'trigger warnings' in the last few years over lectures on texts which might cause 'distress.' But Northampton University took the biscuit when it issued a trigger for Orwell's 'Nineteen Eighty-four' explaining that it contains 'explicit material' that some students might find 'upsetting.' I suspect George Orwell might have found the University of Northampton's stance pretty upsetting being a man who knew the power of words and the power of omitting them. On second thoughts, he might have said 'told you so.' Mark Haddon's novel 'The Curious Incident of the Dog in the Night Time' written in 2003 was triggered by the same University on the grounds that it depicted 'the death of an animal.'

'My God, when I read that I thought of dear old Izzy. It's too awful. I had to stop reading.' No, it's not really about a dog, but then you'll never know that will you? Oxford University Law students are warned before lectures which might detail 'sexual abuse' that they may leave or skip the lecture. One wonders how these same students are going to cope in the real world when they encounter cases of abuse. Mary Beard the historian wonders how a study of Roman history could be followed without references to rape and animal abuse. 'Today we're going to learn about the Coliseum folks and there will be a wee bit about animal abuse…no, come on, don't leave!' Too late. Can't take it mate. Just can't listen to things that make me feel uncomfortable because I need to feel, like, comfortable.

It's not really a matter of feeling comfortable though, rather it's a matter of learning what a cruel place the world can be and the things that human beings do to each other. Taken to its logical conclusion the 'trigger warning' if acceptable as an excuse to avoid a lecture or discussing a work of literature is in the main censorship. The revisionism that deletes the word 'nigger' from works when that word was justifiable in the context of another age is an offshoot of this dangerous drift which in our universities sees student power asserting itself over traditional attitudes to 'learning.' When Universities become businesses, as many of them have in Britain, now that students are paying fees, the customer becomes the king and he/she calls the shots. In the brave new world of customer power, who will decide the texts that are acceptable?

Anyone who reads extensively has developed a pretty shock-free attitude to what they read. For some a lecture on child-abuse may be too close-to-home, but for others it will lead to understanding. It may not be 'comfortable' watching Julius Caesar being cut to ribbons but that's what happened. Reading To Kill a Mockingbird may not be 'comfortable' but it highlighted the issue of racism in the Deep South. Reading 'Kim', Kipling's novel, doesn't make you a complicit Imperialist—it offers an exploration of the issues thrown up by Imperialism. What avoiding the unpleasantness of life or disregarding history makes you, is a person without understanding, without compassion, without curiosity, without the tools to handle life's cruelties. In short it makes you the kind of person who writes into 'Poetry Please' asking for a nice poem about

trees or a listener to Classic FM who craves 'relaxing'
music. Ostensibly there's nothing wrong with that,
but I personally feel uncomfortable hearing about a
tree that might be cut down.

Don't be offended, just fuck off back under your
stone, I say, but then I can be quite offensive at
times. Old and offensive. Be warned. Oh, too late,
should've issued a trigger warning.

26.

Today the 'gas-man' is coming* to install a new meter. Panic begins to rise in my breast. Every time anyone enters the house with the task of doing something practical my first reaction is to flee. I'm not a practical man. I know nothing of gas or electricity or boilers or where cables should go and where they shouldn't. It's not that those who do aren't pleasant people, it's just that they have a tendency to assume I know things that I don't (because I'm a man!) and to ask questions that I can't answer. 'When was your boiler last checked?'

'Er…last year?'

'Yes, but when, exactly?'

'I'll get my wife.' She's not really my wife but why get into that.

And she who is not my wife can usually answer these questions.

Now I'm not being a superior wee shit here who thinks such things are beneath me. No. I would quite like to be able to answer their questions, it's just that I'm not really interested enough to find out. Anything that doesn't have a working heart and preferably skin, doesn't float my boat as they say everywhere. The fact that we live in an increasingly technical age is bad news for such as me. Yes, I have a mobile phone (is it OK to call it that?), and yes in a limited way I use it to arrange golf on What's App and occasionally phone my partner but if I could function in this society without the damn thing, I would. When I see other people totally fixated on their phones to the exclusion of the world about them, I despair. Out walking it's the same. Someone will approach me at a trot, and I set myself for a 'Hi' or a 'Morning' and they pass, jogging along, those white earphones in, without a glance in my direction. Never be without your music or you might die, seems to be the order of the day, a bit like that craze for water bottles a few years ago when if you went for a twenty-minute walk without one you might die of dehydration. Never be without some artificial means of stimulation. Don't just run for the sake of running but listen to James Corden's Car-pool Karaoke while you run. One of these days the eminently annoying Corden's going to be going for a ride with Jesus and they'll be driving along singing 'Bringing in the Sheaves.' But technology doesn't just bugger the purity of running, it can also bugger the purity of an evening out for a meal.

Don't know how often I've sat in a restaurant and watched a couple at another table looking at their phones—he on one side —she on the other, with never a word exchanged till the pizza arrives. Pizza! Now that's for another day. Under the guise of connecting us, the remoteness that technology affords can take us into dangerous territory. Scams by phone are on the increase, and by using the phone as a tool to meet others we can lay ourselves open to abuse. 'You look nice—send me a picture of your boobs.'

Last evening, I watched a documentary film called 'Tinder Swindler' in which several young women had, unknowingly, linked up to the same man on Tinder, the dating site. On the screen the photograph of a good-looking young man with his very expensive car and another of him in his very expensive private plane. Well, what's not to like girls? So, they get in touch, and they go on a date, and he wines and dines them and shows each of them a jolly good time and they fall in love with him, and he makes love to them. Trouble was, none of them realised the others existed. Then one day during deep and meaningful text exchanges such as 'Miss you.' and 'Love you.' and 'Want to have your babies', said lover sends a photo of his 'minder' who's just been beaten up. Lover says he's in danger and to cut a longer story short—he needs money. The girls borrow money to give him. Lover gets lots and lots of money from the ladies who never get it back. Each lady is paying for the flashy cars and the plane and the meals of the other ladies. Now why am I telling this? Because much of what happened here took place by phone. Much of what happened was a lie. And money was sent by phone. 'Tinder' and other dating sites leave folk exposed to swindlers such as this man. If he hadn't been dashing all over the place and each had spent more time with him talking, maybe they would have rumbled him. Unbelievably he spent only five months in an Israeli prison and is now out and about again while the ladies are left repaying their debts. Today we're able to engage with each other remotely with all the risks attendant on the absence of human contact.

What happened to conversation? What happened to greeting another human being as you pass? And what is it doing to us, all this technology? It's drawn a whole generation or two into themselves, oblivious of others. It's made my partner an obsessive I-pad user. For hours on end, it seems to me, she scrawls through Facebook looking at pictures of Labradoodles running on beaches, or whales who have landed on beaches presumably seeking labradoodles and now can't get back into the sea, or elephants rescuing their babies from river banks. And when that's all done there's the New York Times crossword or Wordle to keep her interest in the world. She has lost the ability to focus on a film without multi-tasking with the I-pad. She'd deny all this of course, but this is my perception and I'm doing the writing. I-pads, phones, and an area that is completely alien to me—games.

I pass a house on my walk with the dog (yes, she's a labradoodle) and every evening I glance into a room with a huge television on which racing cars are charging round a track or funny little figures are being blasted to Kingdom come. I see the head of a young boy and he's obviously playing a game, completely and utterly absorbed. I wonder how many hours he spends doing this and to what end? Amusement?

The only outcome from the hours spent doing this is an increased ability to do it, but if the game has no value as a human experience isn't it a waste of time? Oh, that's my partner back form the dentist and luckily the gas man hasn't come yet. She'll deal with him, and I'll get on my Apple Mac and type this. Might even have a game of chess.

PS. * the gas man didn't come.

27.

Louis Theroux's piece in The Guardian today is trailing his upcoming TV series in which he interviews supporters of America's Hard Right and other assorted groups, though such a mainstream political description as 'Hard Right' flatters the adherents of these factions with a degree of intelligence which their rantings contradict. If there is a spectrum of political belief, then the position of 'Millenialism' or 'Antinomialism' is as far from Marxism as Kensington is from Ferguslie Park in Paisley. The folk the benign Louis will be interviewing are those who believe in the power of lizards to invest the bodies of those they detest and who think Trump was much too woolly in his views to effect real change. These guys make Frankie Boyle's rantings sound like a bedtime story.

Give your run of the mill US Republican senator a t-shirt with 'Hate' emblazoned on it in blood-red, a cap with something a little more violent on it (oh come on, try!) and offer him an assault rifle and he just might join the club. But then, though his grasp of the world may be tenuous and his moral compass in an attic somewhere, he would still be overqualified to join this gang.

To join these gangs you need to be a 'believer.' You believe that Armageddon is just round the corner and you've got your stores in and your guns cocked ready to defend yourself from the ravaging hordes searching for a grain or two of rice. Or if you've never heard of Armageddon, don't fret, there are others that might just be worth a subscription—The Proud Boys,

The Three Percenters, The Oath Keepers or Q Anon. Take your pick. Whoever you hate, there's a place for you in the ranks— Jews, The Government, Gays, Women, Raped women who want an abortion? Just sign here.

Look, we all like to belong, don't we? Most of us belong to things like the church choir, or the boy scouts, or the golf club, or the rotary, and most of us are content. Most of us had parents that loved us and only beat us up when necessary. We grew up in the belief that being nice to people is just what nice people do. But what if you're growing up is a bit more full-on? What if you grew up in the middle of America miles from the nearest town and didn't have parents or your parents were alcoholics or drug addicts or even brother and sister. What if living in a shit little town was all you had to look forward to and there were no jobs? What if you were bored by school and spent your days playing video games and eating Ritz Crackers and one day you tuned into a Trump rally and this big guy with cool hair told you how shitty your life was and who was to blame? What if he told you how to fix it and you believed him. What if he told you, it was Black people and Muslims and Mexicans and gay people and Jewish people and so on that were the cause of your shitty life? How would you feel? Would you be angry? Damn right you would. If you didn't have the education to filter truth from lies.

What lies at the heart of adherence to these groups whether Neo-Nazi, White Supremacist or any other, is firstly, a discontent, a sense of disenfranchisement, and secondly and concomitantly, a deep sense of hatred. The objects of the hatred have already been listed—what they all have in common is a focus, a target, the destruction of what lies in the way of your happiness. Kill off The Blacks and you're chances of a job will be better. Kill the Jews because they run business and steal money from poor folk like you. Kill homosexuals because the bible tells you to do it, though you can't find the actual words, and you are a good Christian. Kill in the name of some mythical nirvana that will turn your miserable life around.

America has always had issues with race, to put it mildly. To many in the South, the loss of the civil war was a slap in the face to their notion of the superiority of the white race over the black. And one hundred and fifty-seven years after slavery was abolished, the legacy lives on for some. The murder of George Floyd saw demonstrations against police brutality towards Black men and women and encouraged Black men and women to relate this to the racism they encounter daily. The Covid pandemic only served to highlight that the economic disparity between Black and White in cities across America left them more vulnerable to the disease than White folk. The removal of Statues of Confederate generals in some cities as a gesture of solidarity with the Black Lives Matter campaign may be seen as a positive gesture but it has also been seen by racist-motivated groups as a challenge. If you see Black people as a threat and support for them seems to be in the ascendent then it's time you did something about it.

In recent times White Supremacist Groups have ditched their traditional regalia to be seen as intellectually respectable—a part of mainstream politics. If you want a voice in Congress, it might be inadvisable to drape yourself in a swastika, even if you are a Republican. And if you crave some sense of stability then you are likely to latch on to any reason for your instability no matter how absurd it may seem to more rational minds. It's a conspiracy.

Twenty-eight percent of the American population, according to national statistics—that's about eighty-five million people, believe that a Secret Elite Power is trying to rule the world. And four percent believe this power resides in shapeshifting reptile aliens. It's Frankie Boyle again! Contrails are not the crystalising of water droplets but the government spraying the population with mind-shifting chemicals. And here's a beauty-- 'Birds Aren't Real' placards—there are no birds: those little things with wings are really drones watching over us. Add a few beliefs about a network of underground tunnels manned by aliens and lizards out to get us and a paedophile conspiracy out to do God-Knows-What and you have a sprinkling of the conspiracy theories believed by millions of Americans today. Many of these beliefs are disseminated on certain radio stations, on the web or The Dark Web, and their aims are clear— cause discontent, spread fear and stimulate mistrust. In a society awash with weapons such beliefs are the tinder from which fires arise. If there are two ideologies that might be said to be at the heart of America's dystopian condition it would be the gun as protection and God as justification.

The Bill of Rights ratified by Congress in 1791 included the words '…the right of the people to keep and bear arms shall not be infringed.' It gave the people 'the means and ability to rebel against a tyrannical government.' It symbolised power and protection against oppressors. Two hundred and Thirty Years later many Americans still cling to their 'rights'. Guns are everywhere and the further Right you are, the more you feel the need to be armed against what you perceive as an anti-white, anti-Christian power structure. You have the gun in one hand and God in your heart.

When Donald Trump stood in front of St John's Episcopal Church in Washington on the second of June 2020, in the aftermath of a brutal police action against mostly peaceful Black Lives Matter protesters, he had in his hand not a gun, but a bible. It was a symbol for him of an age-old connection between racism and God. The KKK's burning cross symbol, a throwback to ancient European practices warning of imminent attack, came to represent their 'faith in Christ.' Trump's gesture, from a man whose affinity with love and any other Christian virtues would be difficult to discern, was a kind of spiritual porn, a theatrical display for those who see the secularisation of America as a threat to everything they believe in.

Thomas Jefferson, the author of the American Constitution and the Third President, wrote in a letter to his nephew Peter Carr to… 'Shake off all the fears of servile prejudices, under which weak minds are servilely crouched. Fix reason firmly in her seat and call on her tribunal for every fact, every opinion. Question with boldness even the existence of a God; because if there be one, he must more approve of the homage of reason than that of blindfold fear.' Jefferson may have had doubts about a deity, but he had none about the importance of 'reason'. Neither reason nor clear thinking but adherence to the gun and God are the twin pathologies of almost every right wing, extremist organisation in America today and Theroux's brave exposure of their beliefs should not, as some might claim, be seen to be giving these beliefs oxygen, but in fact exposing ignorance and prejudice for what it is. Better that the extremists' faces are shown and that their beliefs are challenged face to face.

The underbelly of any society has always existed but today perhaps more than at any other time, modern media enables lies and misinformation to be accessed by those whose critical faculties, dulled by indoctrination or poor education, believe they are being cheated of a good life and need someone to blame—need a cause to adhere to. In the past we knew little of the extremists, till Donald Trump appeared and his populist anti-establishment message gave voice to the millions in America who had seemed silent. Trump would 'drain the swamp' that was Washington. That many million Americans believe that the election of Joe Biden was fraudulent is testament to the central issue in many Western Democracies today—how can we tell truth from lies when we are besieged from all directions by the white sound of politicians who bandy statistics that are beyond our means to verify? In Britain we have our own stranger to the truth, who exposed as such, is as reluctant to relinquish his power as was Trump. We shall see. We shall see.

28.

Reading Dawkins' 'The God Delusion.' I have a sore neck from nodding as he tilts at the absurdities as he sees them, of conventional religious belief. From an early age I think I failed to be fertile soil for belief. It wasn't that my super brain at age twelve had shredded the Gordian knot of Christian teaching, rather that it was all a bit of a bore. Sunday meant Church, and Church meant suffering.

Attending Church on a Sunday and my father being an 'elder,' I'd watch him troop down the aisle with a few others, plates brimming with collection envelopes (there's discretion for you!) to deliver them to the minister. I can't remember when the 'sermon' came, but when it did, after a couple of hymns, which I would happily belt out, a dread descended. This was going to be twenty minutes or more of gobbledygook for me and I knew for my old man too. The Rev Mathieson would quote from the writings of men my father had never heard of such as Bertrand Russell or Dietrich Bonhoeffer and throw in a letter Paul wrote to the Corinthians one sunny morning in Tarsus. 'Hi guys, I've a few points I'd like to make about 'love.' It was as if up there in his pulpit he was on another plane and his job was to justify his position by completely bewildering the poor folk who had to sit on these hard pews every Sunday. It was as if the sermon was the price they paid for being believers.

Now I would look at my father's face as this was going on and watch his cheeks move as he played tennis with the pan-drop dissolving in his mouth. I think the pan-drop probably kept attendances up, for without it The Church of Scotland pews would have been empty. For me, the penny dropped too. Bugger this for a laugh I thought, and thankfully my attachment to religion was on a very loose leash.

I think I'm so far out of the loop as far as religion goes that those moments on the radio still reserved on a Sunday for a Church Service or the daily talk by The Reverend Joe-soap of The Church of Latter-Day Elephants has me blasting the order at Alexa to 'Stop!' The emergence of the 'happy-clapper' syndrome, where a bunch of youthful worshippers bring along their guitars and strum their way to Heaven seems to me to be a desperate attempt to attract an audience that is only waiting impatiently for their church to become the latest Weatherspoon's. Church after church seems to have succumbed as attendances plummet. Only seven percent of Scotland's population attends Church regularly, a mere 390,000— forty-two percent of which are over sixty-five. Now I don't know why this decline has happened or whether pan-drops are in short supply, but in the last thirty years or so we are entering a new age of secularism in Britain where spiritual guidance such as it was, is no longer felt relevant to today's world.

The Greek philosopher Epicurus wrote, "Men, believing in myths, will always fear something terrible, everlasting punishment as certain or probable... Men base all these fears not on mature opinions, but on irrational fancies, that they are more disturbed by fear of the unknown than by facing facts. Peace of mind lies in being delivered from all these fears.' 'Reason' and 'fact' seem to be under attack in our society and others.

While I side with Dawkins and Charles Darwin and the 'Big Bang' theorists as opposed to those who believe in an 'intelligent Creator,' it's problematic to blame a specific religion for those who hide behind it or interpret its precepts as a reason to hate others. Most religions preach 'love' but that's too simple for those that have issues with others. We're human, unfortunately. If we hadn't invented Gods and prophets, we'd probably have found other pretexts for conflict. Folk with blue eyes hating folk with green eyes: folk with brown hair hating folk with ginger hair and so on. Well Hitler found it quite easy to whip up hatred for a whole race and we know where that led. Wasn't that about hair colour and noses as much as about Jewish financial dealings? You must be able to spot your enemy and if he wears certain clothes or has any other distinguishing features then so much the better.

But while religion can be divisive between nations and within multi-cultural societies, the strict rules of many religions play a part in governing conduct. If you believe that 'doing good' or shall we say 'not doing bad' has some reward in an after-life, then why wouldn't you adhere to the rules? If there are no rules, what guides you?

To the non-believer some of these rules seem absurd.

Hasidic teaching is essentially built on the stricture to 'change nothing'—that is, change nothing from the way the group behaved in Eastern Europe in the eighteenth century. Clothes, food, hair, transport, sexual habits, in fact all aspects of life must remain unaltered. And while for most, indoctrinated at an early age to conform, this presents a firm stencil for a well-lived life, for those on the outside it feels like repression—a denial of the pleasures of the world in the twenty-first century. Women everywhere in the West still struggle for equality with men in all aspects of life but the Hasidic woman's role as in some other religions is essentially that of wife and mother—nothing else. You shave your head, and you wear a wig. You don't worship in the same space as men and your husband is chosen through negotiation. For several days each month while the wife is menstruating the couple must not touch each other. Before marriage, neither sex has any experience of intimacy. On your wedding night you may need one of the manuals on offer. Religion for the 'sect' is a way of life, while for those who sit in the pews of The Church of Scotland or England, it can often be little more than two hours out of your week listening to a man wearing a dog-collar. When you exit with a handshake you resume your secular life.

While I read Dawkin's crusading work with a nod, something in me stirred, and that was the feeling that ditching all that belief as being irrational and essentially pointless, leaves us with a hole which every society that ever existed has filled with some spiritual belief. Mankind always seems to need to worship something greater than himself. When you strip away the rituals, the priests, the buildings, why you even ditch Sunday as a special day, what is left? The poet Philip Larkin wondered that too.

In 'Church Going' he accepts this need that people have, to question why we are here, and he questions the demise of The Church. Larkin was agnostic, but even he sensed the need, the assurance that existence had some meaning beyond the mundane. He takes off his cycle clips 'in awkward reverence' even though he is a non-believer. If this need is not being met in our secular society, then what do we substitute for it? Amazon? Strictly Come Dancing? Gambling? Netflix? Football? Holidays in Ibiza? A new car? What do we have beyond the material world that might guide our conduct? Is it only that working hard will enable you to buy more things? Are the happiest people those who have everything they want? I doubt it.

Listening to the News as I do, it saddens me when I hear of nurses and doctors being abused by patients, of fire-crews being bombarded as they go about their job, of increasing cases of teachers being abused by their pupils, of the use of the mobile phone as a means of blackmail. I don't think I exaggerate here. In 2019 the police recorded more than nineteen million cases of antisocial behaviour in Britain, a vast increase from 2001.The number of police officers on our streets has declined over the years, the beat 'bobby' being a phenomenon from another age—a man or woman who knew their patch and the folk who lived there and who was, if not a welcome presence for some, for others a reassurance that the law was still awake and listening. But perhaps we should look, not at the police but inside the home for the answer to the problem of anti-social behaviour.

Why does a large and growing minority of predominantly young men seem oblivious to the harm their antics do? Why is it that a concept like 'respect for others' seems beyond some? Is it that the space which would once have been filled by a spiritual dimension has disappeared? Is it that 'belief' has withered in our society and been replaced by envy? Or is this too facile an explanation. From where does the anger that exhibits itself in anti-social behaviour emanate?

Most of those young men come from areas of deprivation where schools are poorly financed, and jobs are in short supply. Boredom and an anger that comes from hopelessness, too often spills over as abuse of those in any kind of authority. Good parents know where their children are—poor parents don't care. As jobs disappear in communities, so does hope and respect—self-respect. A man who has no sense of himself will have no sense of others. There are no rewards for being good but there may be some fun in being bad. Today our society is changing. Many children are without a mother or father as the concept of the nuclear family declines. The voices that guided the children are either absent or diminished. No-one is watching. No-one is there to pat you on the back for not taking that drug. No-one is there to encourage you to go and learn a skill. No-one is there to be proud of you and to make you proud of yourself.

I have no recollection of this degree of abuse towards authority as I grew up in the fifties and sixties, but it was a different world. Teachers have always had pupils who were bored but they didn't have mobile phones that could video them in their less-than-perfect pedagogic moments. Doctors and nurses were never abused to the extent they are now, and firemen put out their fires and were applauded as they did so. But that was then, when some might argue religion played a more active role in our lives and policemen walked the streets. Norms of conduct were generally adhered to by all members of society and drugs hadn't been invented. But while it's tempting to go down this road, blaming secularism, extensive research has shown just the opposite: that a secular society is likely to have less crime than a religious one.

Incidence of crime in the Southern States of the USA where religious belief is strong, is greater than crime above the Mason-Dixon line. Perhaps there is an obvious answer here and it lies not in religious belief but simply in standards of living. The standard of living in the North of America is higher than that in the God-fearing South and the precepts of belief which might determine attitudes and consequently conduct are much less stringent. The God-fearing South still clings to a God who hates homosexuals, who abhors abortion, who fundamentalists believe favours the white man over the black. And beliefs such as these in a 'modern forward-looking society' will often lead to criminal behaviour. While some of Europe's 'secular' societies (perhaps non-churchgoing would be more accurate) such as France, Belgium, Netherlands and Germany have low crime rates; a country like Spain with a strong religious tradition has a much lower crime-rate than 'secular' Britain.

The deeper one delves into the religious/secular debate the clearer the water becomes.

It is not religious belief which determines a country's crime-rate but the standard of living of its citizens. If a society cares for its people—all of its citizens, then crime will be lower than in one which does not. Britain's crime-rate is almost the highest in Europe and the huge gulf in living standards not just between the North and South of England, but between the 'haves' and 'have-not's' manifests itself in the hopelessness and anger mentioned earlier.

The Tory Government proudly boasts that it is building more prisons. What does this say about our society? That we are less tolerant of crime? No. It says that we have a government that will not see the causes of crime and anti-social behaviour because that would demand they question themselves about equality—about how much Britain cares for its poorest citizens.

In fifty years, the face of Britain has changed. Margaret Thatcher ('...who is society? There's no such thing...') killed the coalfields long before Global Warming and fossil fuels were on the agenda. She sold off council housing, leaving whole generations of young people struggling to put a roof over their heads. She de-industrialised Britain turning it into a service- economy where the dignity of labour was reduced to working in a Call-centre.

St Paul's Letter to the Corinthians:

'Love is patient, love is kind. It is not jealous, is not pompous,
it is not inflated, it is not rude, it does not seek its
own interests, it is not quick-tempered, it does not

brood over injury, it does not rejoice over wrongdoing but rejoices with the truth.'

The 'TRUTH.' Johnson, are you listening?

29.

Blue sky but cold. I like it.

Too early for bed and channel hopping after Newsnight, I settled on 'Naked Attraction.' Being male and heterosexual I'm not averse to watching a naked woman or two when the occasion arises. Here was a good-looking woman in her early sixties on a game show where she chooses a 'date' by scrutinising the naked bodies of six men then has to appear naked before the last two she picks. I believe she was an Australian dentist. She was obviously 'up for it' as the saying goes, demonstrating her fellatio technique on a peeled banana. Licking down the shaft and then circling what would be the glans with her tongue. The show's madam (sorry, compere) was very impressed. Presumably if and when the latter does this, she just sucks very hard and hadn't thought about licking at all. Well, the coloured booths revealed their specimens of manhood from the bottom up till legs assessed and willies assessed the heads were revealed and encouraged to justify being chosen. Two were left standing and then our dentist emerged naked to be scrutinised in turn by the men. I think one was a plumber and the other another tradesman of some sort. The lady had a good look and made the choice of her date. Jump to the lady and the gent sitting fully dressed on their date in some bar. Jump to inane chat about how good each was looking. Then back to the final judgement— will you both be meeting again? Lady sitting on a sofa. Unfortunately, gent had declined to turn up. Ha.

If you'd described this programme to me twenty years ago, which isn't that long in the past, I'd have laughed. Folk naked? You're joking. And they choose a date from a naked person? You are having me on. Never. You'd never see this on TV. But we do.

Apart from the obviously idiotic notion that we choose partners by assessing their genitals, which in many cases we don't see till we have decided that we want to spend time with them, the elimination of other factors such as class, intellect and interests leads randy Australian dentists to go on dates with a penis rather than a brain. Why I should write this at all and be remotely surprised with the disappointing outcome you might wonder. This isn't a rational approach to dating—this is voyeurism in excelsis. We like looking at naked bodies and the makers of this programme know that. So 'society' is sick? Er…no.

It seems that after initial high viewing figures, the British public have had enough of this. The show's advertising on London Transport was banned after complaints. An attempt to make a 'Celebrity Special' where 'celebrities' would expose themselves has been ditched. They couldn't get enough contestants. It would seem that as the show developed, the need to spice things up has gone too far for the British public. Women are appalled at male contestants nodding approbation at 'neat' vaginas. Some even say they don't mind a bit of 'labia.' That's kind of you gentlemen. Jesus. The 'compere' is always eager to know what 'turns on' contestants and some contestants are eager to share. After a while however, 'I like it doggy' or 'don't mind a bit of tongue up the arse' like many things, cease to shock and become plain boring. Shock, like the splash of a stone in water, ends in little ripples. But let's be positive. There is still a vestige of decency left in the viewing masses who see this for what it is—exploitation. That 'celebrities'—those beasts that need publicity to pay the bills—were reluctant to go on the programme, shows that not all exposure is considered profitable. They will gladly swim in a tank of cockroaches or devour cobra pooh on 'I'm a

Celebrity...', but they will not show the public their genitals. I suspect if their genitals could do a good song and dance routine, they just might go for it, but alas.

Well talking of 'alas' or regret, it seems pubic hair has had its day. Hardly a contestant you'll find with much more than stubble in the lower cornfield. Males and females alike are as naked as pre-pubescent children down there. And in place of a bosky member or grotto, some have devised tattoos such as an elephant head whose trunk is...well you can guess. Tattoos are the thing. Males and females who've been inked with heads and names and swirly bits and peacocks and so on. If I'd even been caught drawing a circle on my hand with my biro when I was at school, I'd have been in the Head's room for a lecture on how I was poisoning myself and might die any day.

Tattoos are not a recent invention though: whether inked or painted, warriors in the past were covered in tattoos as were sailors who saw them as a kind of journal of their voyages. In The Hermitage Museum in St Petersburg, you can see mummies of Scythian kings and princesses tattooed to the nines with beasts of all kinds. But that was a spiritual thing. Today's tattoos tend to have little to do with Gods unless Gary's cock is a manifestation of the Godhead.

Surprisingly, over twenty-one percent of employers in Britain today favour their workers sporting tattoos. Private Investigators for instance see tattoos as a way of bonding with their clients as do many in the fashion industry. There does seem to be a dividing line however when we get to the professions such as medicine, law and banking where tattoos are seen as being less than 'professional.' I would rather have sex with a putrefying wombat than with a woman bedecked in tattoos. Just as you're about to come you'd raise your head to notice the name of an ex—'Love you ever Stevie.' Now that's not on, is it?

The way TV develops, if that's the word, to catch the zeitgeist, I don't think the day will be far off when another shock-jock of a programme comes along. We've done nudity for the moment—how about a variation on these endless competitions such as 'The Great British Bake-off' or 'The Great Pottery Throwdown', with 'The Great Operation Sew-up.' Contestants have two hours to complete an operation in a giant operating theatre and bring the patient round. The patient should survive, if possible, to claim the prize —The Golden Tonsils. Can't wait.

Snow yesterday but it has gone now from the streets. A bright sunny day.

30.

Today I was thinking of what traps nostalgia lays for us. When I was a boy, a sick boy, my mother would take me to see the doctor. Now the doctor lived in a very posh house in Shandwick Place in Edinburgh's New Town. You went up a few steps and pushed the bell and were ushered into a large waiting room with huge bow-windows on the street. I remember there was a model Spanish galleon on a table in front of the window and pictures round the walls in gilt frames. This wasn't like the rooms I knew at home at all and I was very impressed. When called, we'd go along the hall and enter a room where the doctor was waiting for us at his desk. He wore an elegant grey suit and had grey hair. He was what I'd now call 'distinguished.' My mother spoke very politely addressing him as 'doctor' every time she spoke. Then, he was a kind of shaman who had all the answers to the ills of life. He looked down your throat and shone his little torch in your ear. He'd tap your chest and back and listen on his stethoscope. Then he'd pronounce the disease and prescribe the cure. He was a doctor, and he was a man to be respected. I suppose, looking back, the awe my mother felt in his presence was part class-consciousness—no one in our family was a doctor or had even gone to university then—and part ignorance, as there was no 'google' then to answer any questions. Doctors were one of those professions that still clung to a mystique that defied question. Earlier in my life I caught Rheumatic fever and was cured by 'a black doctor' as my mother never tired of reminding me. Now the colour of the doctor's skin was important to my mother then, as I suppose to her, he was a rarity. The fact that someone with a black skin had saved my life was so miraculous that she clung to it as a vindication of his race. If she'd asked his religious convictions and been told he was Roman Catholic, I suspect her enthusiasm would have dimmed somewhat. My mother was born in Glasgow of Protestant stock. But that was then, and this is now.

Then, there was no time-limit on patient consultations. There was no limit to home visits even for such conditions as flu or tonsilitis. You picked up the phone and there he'd be at your door the grey-haired doctor, all smiles, carrying his odd-shaped little leather bag and 'Where's the patient?' he'd say as he entered.

Today, in most towns of any size you'll find a Health Centre. Yes, they're a bit like crematoria in construction— built with a functionality that defies any architectural interest whatsoever. You'd be lucky to see a Spanish Galleon and the doctor won't be wearing a nice suit, but you'll be seen, and you will be asked questions and you'll go out the door with a prescription. If you have a chronic condition and your medicine runs out, you only need to phone up to have the Pharmacy make up a new medicine. If you live in Scotland, your prescriptions are free. Now I don't know what happened between the intimacy of that Edinburgh doctor's set-up and the modern Health Service provision, but memory can play tricks. If we ignore the blandness of the modern consulting room—much like the blandness of a lecturer's study in a new University building (I'm sure there will be minimum dimensions prescribed in the plans)—my mother's deference to our doctor and the developments in medical science which have stretched the resources of the NHS, there remains the conviction that the existing NHS provision is a small miracle. It's a take on the aphorism about education— 'Education is what remains when all you've learned has been forgotten.' What remains when nostalgia has been overcome, is the NHS. today. But miracles don't occur without intervention, and in the absence of the Divine sort, successive governments have in the main succeeded in providing their citizens with impressive free heath provision.

Go into the cord-carpeted over-heated space of a two-practice Health Centre with its sad wee palm tree in the corner and the play area for the kiddies and the blonde wood of the chairs and the posters everywhere with warnings about Covid, and you wait to be called by… Yes, I know. Who? Probably not the nice chap you saw last time or the lady you saw the time before that—no, the chances are it's a new face that ushers you into his or her little room. S/he doesn't know you from Adam, but they've got your records on their screen in front of them and they've ten minutes before the next for shaving. They'll listen to you and if you're lucky they'll take your blood pressure or listen to your chest or maybe shine their little torch in the cave of your earhole. It's unlikely you will be touched however and there isn't time for a chat about your diet or whether you take exercise or God forbid, if you're feeling happy. And when he's decided what's wrong, he'll swivel in his chair, have a minute at his computer and then look up his book to see what he should prescribe from page after page of pharmaceuticals. Longing for a grey suit and a gentle smile? Forget it. This is today and that was then. It's not pretty, but it works. It's efficient and if it lacks the 'personal touch' perhaps that's a small price to pay.

People are living longer because medicine has developed drugs or techniques to combat most afflictions. Whether living into your nineties depending on a tower of pills and walking aids and a bath hoist is something to be envied, may be a question best left to those who are in the middle of it, but if extended life is the aim, then we've cracked it. My daughter who lives in America sprained her ankle recently. She didn't go to see a doctor as that would have cost her $1000. It's almost inconceivable to the average Briton how much being sick costs in America, and we must do everything possible to retain free health care in Britain.

Our Health Service, after initial inertia, got to grips with the Covid pandemic through vaccinations in a way many other countries envied. Yes, there were issues regarding PPE supplies and the Tory government in a rush and during world-wide

distribution issues gave 'fast track' contracts to some

firms whose

links to the issuers was of dubious integrity. But on

the whole Britain did well in protecting its people

after the initial death toll.

We've come a long way since my boyhood in the

fifties and memory becomes mischievous through

age, but I have another memory.

One day the doctor was called to see me. I was

twelve or so and my biology teacher was an attractive

young woman whose legs had the effect of making

biology seem very attractive. I remember I did a large

drawing of a pair of lungs with labels, and it was on

the wall of my bedroom when the doctor visited. He

noticed it. Mother chirped in, 'Oh, he wants to be a

doctor, doctor.'

He smiled and said, as he lifted his bag, 'Oh I see. Well, I wouldn't recommend it.' You see?

31.

Rain today but mild.

Just watched Stephen Fry on YouTube delivering a scintillating attack on 'political correctness.' This phenomenon seems to me to be effectively illustrated by the response to something said in discussion with the remark 'you can't say that.' If the question is then asked 'Why can't I say that? the answer will be 'You just can't' or 'It's not acceptable today.' Acceptable to whom?

I watched the Monk debate of 2018 which as Fry remarked at one point didn't seem to be on topic but rather became a political jousting match between Right and Left. Fry, covered in a cream suit-- 'dressed' does a disservice to the way his large body and the voluminous garment came together— nevertheless delivered an eloquent attack on the 'toxic, binary, zero-sum madness' as he saw it, of PC. With much faux-apologising for the softness of his 'left' leanings and his plea for '…the primacy of the heart and trust in humanity' he ended with what was his key motivation in opposing PC—the assertion that it didn't work.

Fry argued against the conformity and orthodoxy that PC demands and quoted Bertrand Russell who wrote '…those who feel certainty are stupid and those with any imagination and understanding are filled by doubt and indecision. Let doubt prevail.' If I ever seem certain you can bet there's doubt striving to poke through. Fry believes that change occurs naturally in a society over time and gave Britain's acceptance of homosexuality as an example. PC it seems doesn't want to wait for this 'natural' and hands-off change in attitudes but wants to impose rules on the use of language to fight against what it sees as oppression and prejudice. A divisive approach, as Fry sees it.

I'm with Fry and Russell all the way in opposing orthodox views which impose a kind of uniformity on thought no matter how well intentioned. Like Fry I'm not certain of anything but like to rely on my own sense of decency and rational sense to come to conclusions about things.

His co-opponent of PC, the unsmiling Canadian professor Jordan B. Peterson, not a man I'd want to sit and have a drink with, did make an interesting point concerning the implication behind PC, that we are not individuals but all members of a group. That you play a power-game on behalf of your group. This is a man whose views on gender are somewhat oppressive to women, but here he made the point that in discussion, individual to individual is how it should be. Perhaps there is an underlying agenda to this man's thinking—let's not change anything.

Now we have 'cancel culture' where prominent people whose utterances are opposed for one reason or another are boycotted or in some cases sacked, in order to reinforce the 'norm.' JK Rowling's views on trans men and women transcend scrutiny. It is not whether her views are perceived as essentially harmless or harmful that is the issue: but that in voicing them she's been the subject of so much on-line abuse and threats that she admits her mental health has been affected. She has a right to hold views. She is not advocating harm or hatred. She believes she is supporting many young women who feel at odds with their maturing bodies as she admits she did herself and believes they should not consider sexual re-alignment until they are mature enough to make the best decision possible.

Today, being in the public eye and expressing views contrary to the perceived norm or the accepted stance of a particular sub-group is the equivalent to being in the crosshairs of a rifle waiting to be shot. We are in a world where we all have a voice and many of us like to be heard. As a corollary, many of us don't like to accept opposing views no matter how rationally they are presented. MPs of all parties are now subject to on-line abuse and even death threats when their political views are expressed. It seems that Fry's plea for 'the primacy of the heart' in matters of debate is a cry in the wilderness as far as on-line debate is concerned. The need to punish the controversial is surely a trend that will only end in the silence of the doubters and the triumph of orthodoxy. As the philosopher John Stuart Mill put it, too many voices are a prey to the 'despotism of custom.'

32.

Today, March 2nd, 2022, (a date!) we all love The Ukraine. It's battered buildings and people are there daily on our TV screens. In Parliament today, nearly all MPs wore a yellow and blue ribbon to signal support and the chamber looked up to the gallery to applaud the Ukrainian ambassador. Fine.

Not so fine was Boris Johnson's Tory party which for the last few years has cheerfully accepted donations from Russian oligarchs—those men who have amassed vast wealth at the expense of ordinary Russians by cashing in on oil and gas shares issued by the Yeltsin government in the 1990's. The free-market had come to Russia and the so-called voucher-privatization program of 1992–1994 enabled a handful of young men to become billionaires, specifically by arbitraging the vast difference between old domestic prices for Russian commodities (such as natural gas and oil) and the prices prevailing on the world market. Because they stashed billions of dollars in private Swiss bank accounts rather than in Russian banks, they were hated by the vast majority of the Russian people but were enabled and protected by Government corruption. Some who fell foul of Government expectations were harried and some were murdered. But many co-operated politically and their families moved to The West, particularly London, where they bought property and used its financial institutions to 'launder' their wealth.

Now with the invasion of Ukraine, the Tory party has no option but to freeze the available assets of these men. If you can't fight the Russians on the battlefield the people demand that you fight them some other way and that is by imposing sanctions. Johnson was faced by an irate Ukrainian journalist who accused him of not helping The Ukraine and urging him to implement, a no-fly zone over her country. The somewhat bemused Corn-mop could only respond by explaining that shooting down Russian planes would mean Britain would be at war with Russia. If this seems like turning our back on the Ukraine, in geo-political terms it is a valid response. If Putin gains some confidence from this venture however, a NATO country may be next for shaving. Is he really afraid to drag his country into a nuclear war? If Britain isn't at war with Russia, then her relationship is everything but war.

One wonders what Putin really believes is going to be the outcome of his adventure in Ukraine. When, and in some way he will, militarily defeat the Ukrainian army, what is left? Ukraine in ruins, a population that hates Russia and a country in financial peril at home. Perhaps the one thing which will bring Putin's downfall is khleb—bread, or the lack of it. Surely when a population begins to starve it begins to question the effectiveness of its government. Despite Russia's drive for self-sufficiency in recent years, the programme of sanctions is so robust that even in a few days the rouble has fallen and there are queues at banks to withdraw money. The few radio and TV stations in Russia that dare to question the war have now been shut down. Martial Law may be next. As it is, those displaying the words 'No to War' are liable for prison sentences of up to fifteen years.

Odd things happen in war. Today we saw Biden addressing Congress and belligerently threatening Putin. As one, the whole House rose to applaud him. Republicans especially are all for a good war, aren't they— what they're not so keen on is a good peace. Armaments, anyone?

Noam Chomsky in his book 'The Precipice' published in 2021, writes 'The needs (to avoid war) are far greater at the Russian border, where, as a result of NATO expansion and build- up of forces, accidents with indescribable consequences could easily occur.' Not sure what Chomsky had in mind when he uses the term 'NATO expansion,' but reading that, it almost convinces one that Putin may have some reason to mistrust NATO's spread. Well, of course he does. Most NATO countries are liberal democracies and Russia is certainly not that. I'm not aware of NATO''s 'build-up of forces' rather it seems it's Russia who has done the building up of forces on the border with Ukraine. Chomsky didn't know then what we all know now—that Vladimir Putin was either afraid enough or confident enough to invade a

European country on the pretext of preventing it from joining NATO.

While refugees flee Ukraine into Hungary, Poland and Moldova and weapons and supplies move into Ukraine, we in the 'free' world can only watch and await the outcome. The Baltic States, members of NATO must be praying that this adventure goes horribly wrong for Russia. If it proves a success, then one wonders what Putin will do next. The next time a tank crosses a border, unless it's Moldova or Georgia, Putin will officially be at war with The West.

33.

A cold but bright day. There are still birds in the sky for which we must be thankful.

Went to bed the other night with Putin's warning to The West still in my head about the number of nuclear submarines he had, just waiting to zap us. Unlike some, I've always taken warnings seriously, so I didn't sleep too well waiting for a shudder coming from either Edinburgh or Glasgow or Faslane. I keep

returning to a central issue that I can't shake off—
that one individual seems to have the power to kill
millions. Not for the first time of course. Adolf Hitler
had similar power and we know where that led. But
why as human beings do we allow these narcissistic
psychopaths with their dreamy sense of destiny to
rule over us? Is it merely that the ambition that drives
them outdoes that of those around them or are they
themselves surrounded by less successful
psychopaths?

An examination of the childhoods of many
psychopathic dictators reveals one of abuse by a
father (Stalin and Hitler) and a dysfunctional home
whether through poverty (Putin's family shared some
rooms with two other families) or relationship issues.
Most, as was the case with Ivan the Terrible,
fatherless and bullied by the Boyars, spent an early

childhood learning to defend themselves against bullying. Putin learned judo to protect himself while Saddam Hussein was sent to live with an uncle who gave him a gun. Hitler, wounded as a soldier in WW1 shared many of his countrymen's deep resentment over the terms of The Treaty of Versailles. The victors also harboured resentment and Germany was faced with billions in reparations which led to hyper-inflation in the 1920's—fertile soil, as discontent always is, for the one who can promise a brighter future and has the oratorical skills to persuade his listeners that he has the solutions to their problems. Putin's motivation as a supreme leader is to restore the Empire that was once the USSR before it eventually disintegrated in 1991 under the leadership of the benign Mikhail Gorbachev. If Putin's credo is the reunification of Russian-speaking peoples, then

Hitler's was to absorb German-speaking Aryan people into one super state. Hitler needed lebensraum to create his dream and Putin needs to extend Russia's Western flank to counteract what he sees as the democratic expansion of NATO countries. Putin's enemies are the democracies of The West while Hitler's enemies were The Jews, whom he considered to be partly responsible for Germany's disastrous inflation and the Communists who were non-Aryan Slavs, both groups conveniently deemed untermenschen—sub-human. Putin's assertion that Ukraine needed to be demilitarized and denazified is an eerie and confused echo of history, but then history or the truth depends on who is interpreting it.

E.H. Carr, the Russian scholar and historian's dictum that… 'Geschichte ist ein Dialog zwischen Gegenwart und Vergangenheit' —that history is a dialogue between the past and the present— may be true in the purest sense but I don't think Putin wishes to engage in any dialogue with History that doesn't fit his Worldview. Babi-yar just outside Kyiv was the site of the massacre of over thirty-thousand people, mostly Jews, over two days in September 1941 by the German SS. A menorah today stands as a reminder and Putin's 'Nazis' running Ukraine (whose president Zelenskyy is a Jew) are sensitive enough of these atrocities to maintain this memorial. On March 1st a Russian attack on a nearby radio tower damaged the memorial at Babi yar. For someone who hates Nazis, Putin's forces have an odd way of showing it. One man Hitler, and one man, Putin. But history shows us more examples of how a single individual unchecked, can achieve power through fear.

Saddam Hussein, the authoritarian leader of Iraq, fitted the profile of many psychopathic leaders. He left his mother and abusive stepfather to live with his uncle who presented the young boy with a gun and introduced him to Iraqi Nationalist politics. He was imprisoned for an assassination attempt in 1964 and spent time reading about his heroes Hitler and Stalin. In 1968 the Ba'ath party gained power and Saddam was made second in command of the secret police. From here after more coups his party gained power and he became President of Iraq. It didn't take long for the psychopathic elements of his personality to kick in and any opponents were either imprisoned or executed, the latter taking place in public. Some of the oil wealth of Iraq was spent on social reforms and infrastructure but forty percent of it was spent on arms. The West's mistaken belief that Iraq was making nuclear weapons led to the invasion and the resultant execution in 2006 of the despot.

Whether through poverty, familial disfunction or other cause, it's obvious that these men grew up with little emotional attachment to their families. Madeline Albright the US Secretary of State from 1997-2001 after meeting Putin wrote that he seemed 'so cold as to be almost reptilian.' Joseph Stalin is reputed to have been the cause of the deaths of millions of Soviet citizens. One wonders just how empty of empathy can a human being become who uses the death of others to make themselves happy, to feel fulfilled, to feel safe.

Jon Ronson's book 'The Psychopath Test' is an entertaining and instructive trip through psychopathy in which the writer interviews a number of subjects who tick the recognised boxes as displaying psychopathic qualities. If indeed one percent of the population can be reasonably described as 'psychopaths', then there is one near you.

Westminster, Broadcasting, our prisons and The City are replete with them—the successful ones who have climbed over others to ascend the ladder of politics, the air waves and the CEO's who delight in pointing the finger and saying 'you're fired,' not to mention those who have laughingly ended a life without turning a hair.

When we look around at 'successful' entrepreneurs such as Branson, Gates, Maxwell, Zuckerberg and many others, it's not difficult to determine a 'drive' that has empowered them to riches and privilege. In the neo-liberal marketplace, it's that drive and determination that may motivate some while at the same time laying waste to the lives of those deemed threats to the success of that ambition. Just yesterday the decision was made by P and O ferries to instantly make a workforce of over eight hundred souls redundant and replace them with 'foreign' workers. It was a financial decision we're told. Well, that's a relief then.

Such a decision, if it in any way acknowledges the harm done to the families of these workers, has placed the profit of the Company first and human lives last. So long as the psychopaths rule the world it's not difficult to work out the harm that their lack of empathy and need for self-aggrandisement will cause. Self-delusion, bigotry, racism, and psychopathy in the form of Donald Trump was thought by seventy million American voters to be just what the doctor ordered to 'make America great again.' Just how close America came to becoming ruled by fascism, after the storming of Congress, we'll never know, but that day was surely a warning to all thinking men and women, that in voting one should be 'careful what you vote for.'

Plato discussed the idea of 'the philosopher king' as an ideal ruler. One who had only the good of his people at heart and who ruled through reason. Until we elect men and women who don't want to be important, whose integrity is as sound as it can be, who care about people, we will be ruled by narcissistic psychopaths without empathy whose delusions of grandeur bring only harm to those in their power.

'Moscow does not believe in tears,' is a Russian saying. Vladimir Putin is a subscriber. Perhaps that should be 'Moscow does not believe in reality.'

34.

I've been thinking about 'pop.' Just a wee word that prefixes a host of things which in the main I dislike. Granted, 'pop' is just short for 'popular' and as a man who prefers the unorthodox to the orthodox, I swerve away from the predictable taste of the masses. Ooh, that's so fucking elitist! Don't care.

Pop music doesn't interest me. When I was younger Top of the Pops was all the rage, but as I aged, or as I like to think of it, matured, I liked jazz and 'classical' music best. Have to say though, that The Stones still rock my boat. I just can't get excited about the incessant bass thumping away and the inane lyrics of most modern 'pop' music. If everyone likes it, my urge is not to like it. I think I'm just contrary by nature. But the singing has to be sold and that's where the visuals come in.

The pop video has a lot to answer for. You get three minutes of weird film of singers in wild clothes in fields full of sheep or hanging from scaffolding miming to their latest hit. I wonder sometimes if 'popular' does suggest an absence of quality. As though if something is popular it's accessible whether in art or music and if it's accessible it's probably easy to comprehend. And there's a whole new argument about whether facility is bad, and complexity is good. But let's not get bogged down in my musical tastes. There are other things beginning with pop which keep the horrible flag flying.

A pop-up shop isn't a real shop, a serious shop. It's a fly-by-night, here-today-gone-tomorrow affair that probably pushes inferior goods. The owner isn't sticking around to take back items you don't like. He's gone. Ouch.

How about the vox pop. That technique broadcasters use to find out what the common man in the street thinks about things Naturally a lot depends on what the producers want you to believe. If they interview twenty people who say they're not in favour of the death penalty for speeding but find three who are, then they'll film two of those and one against just to show how much people hate speeding. The Vox pop is a sham in the wrong hands. Hate it.

Pop up on the couch, the doc says before sticking his gloved finger up your rectum. Or just pop your clothes off the nurse says as she prepares to test your heart by sticking little plastic buttons here there and everywhere. Where would the medical profession be without the word pop? 'If you'd just like to clamber up on the table I'll make you scream.' No, I get it. Pop sounds so chummy that you just can't wait to do it.

Women 'pop their cherry' when they have sex for the first time. Maybe they can't wait to do it either. Now I'm not going into the pros or cons of this, but let's just say it's nothing to do with fruit and let's be honest and say I've never been there. End of. Oh, and if I were a woman, I might not like it. Well, not the first time, anyway.

A hot day in Arkansas and you'd fancy a Popsicle. The American lolly. 'It's always Summer with a popsicle.' Lollipop. You see, even we in Britain still cling to the pop of a lolly. Not sure what pop is supposed to connote here, but I'm not a fan of the ice lolly, much prefer the MAGNUM. Now that's a superior lolly. But pop really comes into its own when it's related to time. It's over in a jiffy, just like the pop-up shop.

Another pop I have little liking for is popping the question. Have been married, but don't ever remember doing this. It always seems to me that if you're with a woman for any length of time and you're having sex, you know whether she wants to marry you or not. These idiots that have to make a big song and dance and go down on one knee in a crowded restaurant or climb on stage at the Albert Hall or worse at Old Trafford to propose, I would shoot on sight. 'Oh, will she say yes...' Of course, she'll say yes, that's why she's with you, you idiot. Ok. Pop the question is I suppose, sudden if it's in a place full of folk and they're all watching. And another sudden pop involves Dutch footwear. You've got it. You pop your clogs when you die. You're at the loom one moment then you're underground the next. Pop here was used to refer to pawning the clogs of factory workers in the

North of England. When you don't need your clogs anymore, they can be pawned. 'Pop Goes the Weasel' is the refrain of a song which also uses the pawn idea in an age when money was tight and popping the weasel or stoat (Cockney rhyming slang for coat) was a means of getting from one week to another. Pop. It's all pop. Pop, pop, pop, pop bloody pop. And if you think all of this is going nowhere you can take a pop at me— preferably with your popgun because then it won't hurt too much.

35. Bono (Paul David Hewson).

Trigger warning: if you love U2 don't read this.

A photograph in The Guardian a couple of days ago. Vladimir Putin, Tony Blair and…Bono! All smiles. Wonder if it was a war-mongers reunion and Bono brought out drinks and said something that struck a chord with the other two. Maybe he was telling them what a terrific pair of leaders they were. What he probably wasn't saying was 'Why am I here?' Bono always knows why he's there doesn't he? Bono likes to be in the important photos of our time.

If there is a physical manifestation of ubiquity in the past few years on the World stage, it comes in the form of the multi-coloured-shade-wearing pop star who doesn't even have a proper name. I mean what sort of name is Bono? For a dog perhaps, though even that would be a bit obvious knowing the canine love of a bit of calcium. But a human? Yes, OK it's Bono after Bono Vox a hearing-aid store in Dublin. Yes, he's got a 'good voice.' And yet, there he is— here, there, and everywhere there is fame, in whatever guise. His band is called U2 and that's surely what everyone photographed with him should be asking. 'We know why we're here but you too?" A quick look at photos of Bono with 'celebrities' isn't quick. Here are some…

James Brown

Bill Clinton

Barack Obama

Leonardo DiCaprio

David Bowie

Brad Pitt

George Bush and his daddy

Shimon Peres

Tony Blair

Vladimir Putin…(no, it's true)

Oh and so many more.

I really believe if there is a second coming then there he'll be, smiling behind the shades as he shakes hands with The Messiah.

But let's not be cruel to Bono. There are two sides to this coin. If he's there with all those people, then he must have been invited. The question then arises—why invite a musician into your photo-shot if you're President of the USA? And the answer surely is 'added value.' I may be the leader of the Free World but look who my buddy is. See how in-tune I am with the vibe. It's a variation on 'virtue signalling' called 'COOL signalling.'

At the St Patrick's day lunch in the White House on Thursday 17th March the Speaker Nancy Pelosi, just to make the occasion more Irish, read out a poem written by… you've guessed it— Bono, about the war in Ukraine. It likens snakes in Ireland to snakes in the Ukraine, a stunningly appropriate comparison on St Patrick's day. And it rhymes. Well, sort of, cause that's what poems do, right? If it isn't the worst poem ever written it's on the shortlist and is presently an object of derision on TV in America and in Ireland. You see, when you have a celebration of Ireland you have

Bono. Pelosi may be a good Speaker but if she thought that was a good poem, she left her literary judgement at home. To be fair, she seemed a little embarrassed as if she had to read it because it had been sent by Bono and almost begged the room for some positive feedback. They applauded with the lack of conviction found in a one-armed man.

Now I don't know much about U2's music and I don't need to, other than that there is a social element to their songs. But that's not what this is about—it's about a multi-millionaire musician who uses his fame to ostensibly preach about peace in the world and aid to Africa but really just enjoys being with famous people. I mean we ALL care about starving people, don't we? Preaching can only be taken so far before it becomes boring. I know this because I was taken to Church as a youngster and that put me off religion for life. Playing a guitar and singing songs should not be the qualification for becoming the guru of a generation's conscience and yet the great and the good play into this. There are more worthy Gurus out there such as Noam Chomsky, a man who's actually got a university degree or two. Bono's thoughts on famine are interesting if a little lacking in political depth. To say as he has, that 'capitalism has taken more people out of poverty than any other 'ism' even with a rider or two to protect his rear, seems to be a denial of the whole concept of neo-liberalism. Chomsky defines this dogma, begun in the 70's, as '…undermining mechanisms of social solidarity.' He maintains that the neoliberal concept of 'freedom' is a …'subordination to the decisions of concentrated unaccountable private power.' The rich conglomerates, multinationals and bankers get richer while the people get poorer. And when people get poor, they need foodbanks in order to feed their children. How about another Live Aid for the starving here at home?

If you don't quite get this, then perhaps you need to read a bit more, Bono.

Fame together with exposure, have become the God's of our media age—the age of 'celebrity'— and because millions like your music or your films is no reason to pontificate on matters beyond your understanding. 'Live Aid' did indeed make over $127million and helped famine relief in Africa. It got Geldof a knighthood, entertained millions and gave musicians a stage together, but being on that stage doesn't make you a moral guru.

There are famous people I would gladly listen to on moral matters, acknowledging that their lives or writings offer a view of the world beyond anything I could imagine. I might cite the late Bishop Tutu or Nelson Mandela, Elie Wiesel, writers and intellectuals such as Tolstoy (who also organised famine relief), Orwell, Wittgenstein, Kafka, Steinbeck, Chekhov, Didion, Sontag and Huxley to name a few. Now I read these men and women and I believe their work entitles them to be listened to and understood as offering a moral view of the times.

Bono, stick to the music. Please. And keep out of the frame just for five minutes. Oh, and no more poems.

PS. Heard him on 'Desert Island Discs' and he seemed a pleasant man but then I never doubted it.

36.

The High of the last two weeks has been replaced by
a low. Much colder with today a sleet shower which
scared little Mabel the Bedlington whom we are
caring for this week.

An article in The Guardian today by Mikhail Shishkin
the Russian novelist in which he asks an interesting
question concerning Russia: 'Do a dictatorship and a
dictator give birth to a slave population or does a
slave population give birth to a dictatorship and a
dictator?'

He cites the Revolution of 1919 and the late eighties Glasnost policy of Gorbachev as attempts which failed to bring democracy to Russia. The sixties and seventies saw a failing 'command economy' trying to industrialise an agrarian one but turning peasants into 'workers' was only a first step to turning workers into computer scientists, service-providers and post-industrial innovators. The last transition failed, and Gorbachev's reforms only led to a call from Russia's satellites for more freedom. Shishkin asserts that 'a small number of my compatriots are ready for life in a democratic society, but the overwhelming majority still bow before power and accept the patrimonial way of life.' I suppose 'accepting' a regime and trying to avoid fifteen years in prison does raise the question of what 'accepting' means. Voices which question the regime have been silenced in the Media, so that the 'truth' issued by the regime becomes the only truth available. An Orwellian world of 'doublethink and 'Newspeak' now exists in Russia where the conflict in Ukraine becomes a 'military operation' rather than what it undoubtedly is—an invasion, and thence— a war.

We in the West are heartened to see Russian protesters holding up their 'no war' placards or even their A4 sheets (holding a blank piece of paper will also get you arrested) but the bravery of those few is nothing to the seeming acquiescence of the multitudes that accept the Kremlin's 'truth' or are too afraid to speak out against it. I wonder sometimes why we assume vast swathes of a population care deeply about 'the truth.' Is it not an abstract notion that only becomes an issue when our daily lives are jolted in some way by its effects? Demonstrations against the war in Iraq attracted thousands of marchers through our cities, but majority of the population stayed at home. Their voices were never heard, just as the voices of the Russian people today are not being heard. We watched as the 'Shock and Awe' of the U.S. blew Bagdad apart but like the bombardment of Ukraine it was a TV experience, and we were told it was necessary to protect us. We were told. We were told and we believed. Lies and half-truths are not the exclusive preserve of autocracies.

We in Britain have the ballot box through which our voices can be heard, but that is only every five years. Many indiscretions can be committed by a government in that time and the only outlet for protest is the demonstration. When a government turns its mind to legislating against protest, democracy is under threat. And such a threat exists in our own democracy.

The Police, Crime, Sentencing and Courts Bill of 2021 does just this, under the guise of protecting the population against the inconvenience that many protests cause. The disruptive tactics were said 'to cause a disproportionate impact on surrounding communities and were a drain on public funds.' Is 'a drain on public funds' a valid excuse to interfere with the right to protest? Presumably protests in Russia at the moment are a drain on public funds when hundreds of police are required to arrest people for saying 'No to War.' We must be very careful to judge the danger behind what may seem reasonable words when it comes to a Bill concerned with protest. After all, the most effective protests are probably the most disruptive. The suffragettes disrupted public meetings, set post boxes and buildings on fire and generally made a complete nuisance of themselves no to mention what they did to the Derby. They were successful. What the above Bill fails to realise is that heavy-handed police action or imprisonment can be to the advantage of a cause rather than quell it, if, that is, the intention behind the Bill is to dissuade protest.

While we in the West take our freedoms for granted, we shouldn't imagine we are living in a land of milk and honey. Twisting the truth when the bald truth is inconvenient is a talent cherished by most of our own politicians. 'Never answer a question' seems to be one of the fundamental principles of the Media interview. Just trot out another line and stick to it, and if your line is catchy so much the better. Corn-mop is, if not a master, as adroit as anyone at this game. 'Get Brexit done' was a beauty, and enough to take us out of the club into an imaginary 'sunlit upland' where all those pesky EU regulations could be ditched.

As P and O sacks their crews to be replaced with others earning an average wage of £5 per hour in order to 'save' the company, the Tory party is embarrassed by the decision which is merely an example of a dogma many of them follow— it's the 'free market' in operation, guys. In the Neo-liberal world, the company and its shareholders is more important than the welfare of its workers. You will travel a long way before you hear a politician admit that they were wrong, and yet for me such an admission would be a glimpse into a soul that is not completely sullied by artifice. While Shishkin rightly points out the apparent acceptance of his people to bow down to Putin's 'truth', we would do well to remain vigilant that our own freedoms are not taken from us.

Corn-mop's attempt to prorogue Parliament on Aug 28th 2019 was eventually declared 'unlawful' by the Supreme Court. Johnson had attempted to shut down Parliament for five weeks, leaving only 17days to discuss the Brexit Bill—a warning to all of us that the Government were not averse to using its power to curtail debate in the Commons.

Whether the Russian people are a 'slave people' by nature or have been made one by their system of government, what is clear is that autocratic rule has been the norm in Russia since the first Tsar. Peter the Great dragged Russia into the modern world in the early 18th Century, but it remained a land firmly ruled by an autocratic leader, and it was an agrarian economy—one that mitigated against industrial development. Britain's Industrial Revolution of the Nineteenth century brought urbanisation and with it a political pressure to overturn the power of the rural aristocracy. With education, the formation of Trade Unions and votes for women a strong Parliamentary Democracy evolved.

In Russia, changes after the Second World War brought fundamental reforms which climaxed in Gorbachev's 'glasnost' of the eighties and early nineties— a loosening of the reins which opened up a degree of privatisation but ultimately led to the disintegration of the USSR. Yeltsin transformed Russia's remaining command economy into a capitalist market economy by implementing the market exchange rate of the rouble, nationwide privatization, and lifting of price controls. These changes led to economic volatility and inflation. His successor was Vladimir Putin, a man who sees the break-up of the Soviet Union as a humiliation brought on by The West. His aim, as he has often stated, is to restore the Russian Empire. He wants to 'make Russia Great again' much as Trump wanted to 'make America Great again' and many in the Conservative party closer to home who would like to 'make Britain great again.' Making anything great 'again' suggests a failure to come to terms with a present reality; a turning back of the clock to a perceived golden age when the golden age is one that exists mostly in the minds of the revisionists or perhaps, we should say, revertists. Nostalgia can be fun but shouldn't be relied on as a basis for present or future policies.

37.

Friendship.

I'm not good at it. As the American poet Walt Whitman said, 'I have learned that to be with those I like is enough.' I subscribe to that.
I envy in a way those who have friends that have been friends since childhood or young adulthood, who still can meet and enjoy each other's company. As I think back to friends I've had, I only think of loss, either through neglect or some other unavoidable occurrence. Neglect is my fault. By it, I mean a failure to play my part in maintaining contact. 'Absence makes the heart grow fonder' has an element of truth when you're in love but in friendship it doesn't work for me.

I think my problem is that I don't miss people enough when I'm not with them. I'll call this 'a problem' if my original admission is true—that I lack some essential ingredient that friendship requires. When they are not with me I don't think about them, wishing we were together again. I have travelled to work with people for years and we got on well together in the car, but now that I've moved away from them, I feel no impulse to maintain our relationship. I suppose as friendship goes, for me it's all in the present and isn't on any continuum that distance and years can bridge. You were my friend then and I liked you and we laughed together but I've moved away and the distance between us has broken my need for your company.

I recently spent a day with a man who was my friend once. We worked together at one time in the distant past and he caught up with me again when he discovered we were living in the same city. We spent evenings in the pub and played tennis.

He's a strange fellow who on the surface is easy enough, though underneath there is a layer of anger that manifests itself at times. He once told me in all seriousness that if his wife were unfaithful, he'd have her killed. I believed he meant it. Now this didn't interfere with our tennis or our shared pints, but such a man was never going to reach my cardiac regions. I moved South and we lost touch till one day he emailed to ask if he could come down and see me. Well of course. We could play golf and tennis and have a few drinks—be friends again.

It didn't take more than a few minutes to make it clear how our friendship had atrophied with absence. I'd published a novel and mentioning it, he drew a piece of paper from his pocket. 'Spelling errors,' he said, triumphantly, 'And you an English teacher too.' Not the response I would have wished from a friend. The weekend went downhill fast. He questioned why I had so many books when I could go to the library. He became irritated by a stuffed toy tiger that I had in my room— 'Why have you got that?' He became irritated when we went for a meal (paid for by me) and I misdirected him to the toilets. At breakfast he declined this and that and the other. We played a round of golf during which his irritation at my offer to make it more competitive (I was losing) was quashed. By this time, I couldn't wait for him to go.

My once 'friend' had turned into someone I couldn't stand. What was my part in this? I've often wondered what made him so disagreeable and can only conclude that it was a throw-away remark I made during our meal when I happened to say, quite truthfully that I preferred the company of women to that of men. I would have thought a reasonable response to that would have been 'Why is that?' But no. Nothing. It wasn't said, obviously, to hurt him, but he took it personally. If he'd asked, I would have said that I found many men uninterested in the arts, whereas I have little interest in shelving or synchro-mesh gearing, whatever that is. He told me he had been diagnosed with hypertension. Now there's a surprise. An angry man and one I can only assume has become deeply insecure. A friend gone unfriendly and not the first.

I've also had issues with friends when my professional duties clashed with their family loyalties. Twice as a teacher I had to issue reprimands to the children of two of my friends and colleagues. There was never in my mind any chance that I would make exceptions in these cases and that ended the friendships. And so it goes.

I think there are several reasons for losing friends: neglect; a clash of loyalties; time; a change of character or ambition on one side that alters the balance; a failure to see the benefits of continuing the relationship; distance apart.

My oldest friend, one with whom I was at school, sent me a mail recently. He lives in the North of England and plays accordion in an accordion band. He was wearing a straw boater in the picture. My initial response was 'Fuck.' Now something told me that this was not the same boy I'd shared so much with. I didn't feel that we had much in common now and that a meeting would only be a disappointment. Can't stand accordions. And the straw hat? Well, if he'd had bells on his legs and been a Morris dancer the effect would have been the same. Distance, time, interests, had all intervened to kill off any chance of a renewal of our good days together. But then, I didn't need it.

I have lost a little faith in people as the years pass, I have to say. I believe essentially most people are selfish. If being with someone doesn't make YOU feel good, you wouldn't do it, though I do acknowledge that sometimes you might sacrifice that feeling to help them in some way in the hope that relations would be restored. A good friendship is only possible if both parties feel the benefit of it. Trust, kindness, understanding, and a degree of selflessness are all necessary to maintain a friendship over time. Added to that you must be able to meet often or correspond often. I wonder how many relationships between the sexes can be maintained over a distance. 'Absence makes the heart grow fonder' may be true for a short time, but the heart needs feeding, and distance doesn't allow that. I suppose if you don't move away from your friends, continuing friendship is no problem but in today's world most people do move and the need for social intercourse remains. When you move you meet new people; people with whom you have no history. They're new to you and you are new to them.

My closest friend now is someone who lives in my town and with whom I've had a friendship for nearly twenty years. We are both ungregarious men. In Whitman's terms it works because I like him. We meet once a week and talk about art. He's an artist and I admire his work. We ask nothing of each other, and I think one of the reasons our friendship has lasted is that we don't challenge each other. We don't do the blokey thing of slagging each other off. We are respectful, unlike my disrespectful visitor. So, I can be a friend and to be honest I'd miss him if our friendship ended. Other friends are the guys I play golf with. This is a sporting friendship and one with limits. We meet on the golf course, play golf and have a few drinks. And that's it. We like each other and are respectful of each other. If we all lived in the same town, I suspect our friendship would develop further, but drink driving laws mean no get-togethers for a beer or two.

By the way, I have 367 friends on Facebook. Not bad, eh? Some friend I am. It's a gift.

38.

Wet again. I love the drip of rain when I'm in bed.

When a woman questioned his lack of hatred for the Southerners in the Civil War, Abraham Lincoln asked, 'Do I not destroy my enemies when I make

them my friends?' It may sound like a nifty piece of wordplay, but the man knew his political onions. Now I'm as troubled as that woman was, in the midst of the mash of hatred, at the prospect of Ukraine's politicians sitting down to discuss peace with their Russian counterparts. I hope the least the Ukrainians can do is to offer the Russians a bus tour of Mariupol as a peace gesture...

General Russki: 'But why Mr Zelenskyy have you destroyed this city? Was it just to make my Motherland look bad in the eyes of the world?'

President Z: 'Oh yes, and didn't I do a good job. There's nothing left. And the world hates you.'

General Russki: 'Being a Nazi, I suppose there's nothing you wouldn't do to fake the truth.'

President Z: 'I see you have a whole breast of medals there General. What's that one for— genocide? And that one—killing children? And that one—shooting missiles into apartment blocks?'

General Russki: 'I didn't come here to be insulted by people like you. I earned these fighting for my country in Chechnya and Syria. Now if you'll excuse me and my delegation who came here to talk peace, we will excuse ourselves. There is no talking to people like you…'

Yes, well something like that. I can't imagine the depth of hatred stored in the hearts of the Ukrainian people for the soldiers that have despoiled their land. But Lincoln is right—without forgiveness, and that is implied in his wish to make friends of his enemies, there can be no resolution. Or can there?

The resolution of The Second World War was the military defeat of Germany. There was no forgiveness for those implicated in the atrocities of the Nazi regime: they were hanged. Perhaps it was the acknowledgment by the people of Germany that those atrocities occurred, that helped a renewal. Most were shocked and ashamed. It has taken at least two generations to erase the sense of National guilt felt by Hitler's actions. Now Germany is at the heart of the European Union and a member of NATO. If the German people knew little of the Death Camps, then the Russian people know little of the war in Ukraine. They are being told lies; Orwellian lies which are food and drink to a controlled Press. It is never The People who start wars, but the rulers of countries and it is never the rulers that suffer during the conflict but The People. For Hitler, read Vladimir Putin. The difference now is that no military offensive is set to defeat Russia. This war is a one-way street. No NATO alliance is going to drive Russia from Ukraine and invade Russia in order to capture Putin and his cronies. No-one in The Kremlin is in danger of being hanged. Why? Two reasons.

Firstly, this is a defensive war on Ukraine's part. There is only one aggressor and that is Russia. The Second World War was also defensive but the defence was able to turn itself into attack. Germany did not possess nuclear weapons. This time that cannot happen.

Secondly, and more importantly, Russia has a nuclear arsenal. Were that not the case, NATO could easily have come to Ukraine's aid and swept the Russians from Ukraine soil. As has been demonstrated, the Russian war machine is a cranky one, with poor morale and poor military thinking. Now having failed to capture Kyiv, they are focusing their attention on the East to partition the Russian-speaking regions of Donetsk and Luhansk as a buffer should Ukraine join NATO. But the Ukrainians are on their own in this conflict because The West believes that Putin would use his nuclear arsenal if forced to do so. We, the sane, peace-lovers, face an insane warmonger who has the power to destroy both us and himself. While Putin stays in power and those around him, the world is not safe. How to remove him and establish a regime with which the West can co-exist is the problem. In 1945 the allied armies brought Hitler down; but no armies will bring Putin down. Peace talks can only resolve this crisis to the advantage of Russia, for that is the only outcome that Putin can possibly accept to keep face. When the Eastern Regions become independent by treaty, Putin will have won a victory; not the one he hoped for, but the victory of arms over Law. One wonders what his next adventure may be.

Putin will never be our friend for we will never defeat him.

39.

I've written before in these Second Thoughts about the psychopathic personality and the effect it can have on others, whether as a war-mongering autocratic leader or as I witnessed last evening, an economic war-mongering tycoon in the bloated shape of Robert Maxwell (Jan Hoch). What both have in common is the driving conviction that life is a jungle. Eat or be eaten. Win or lose. Make a fortune or be poor. Be important or be nothing.

Most of us don't see life that way. We try our best to achieve what we can and settle for a comfortable life. Some however get drawn into the net that such tycoons spread. Maxwell gives you a job, you are delighted for the salary is way above what you ever dreamed of. But you pay. You are a lackey to the whims of the great mogul. When he tells you to do something you jump. You must jump you see, because you've got used to your high salary and you know that one false step and you'll be on your uppers.

'Yes sir, no sir, three bags full sir.'

I watched the film last night and saw the faces of the lackeys as Maxwell delivered his speeches. I knew those faces; they're the same faces that sat round Putin's War-cabinet as he addressed them. Men, (one non-man—there's always a Thatcher who lets the gender down) who had sold their souls and had nowhere to turn now that their boss had become insane. At The Daily Mirror, there were men and women whose gratitude for a nice job outweighed any doubts they had as to the moral convictions of their boss. I wonder if Maxwell's underlings began to have similar doubts to Putin's lackeys as his empire began to crumble. Now I've never been a lackey of that sort. I've never been swept into a net that promised me luxury, so it's easy for me to take the moral high ground and say I'd never allow myself to be ensnared; but I know I wouldn't. And why wouldn't I? Because money has never been the driving force of my life. I've no talent for it. That's probably why I became a teacher. Not much money but a comfortable and satisfying life.

Both Putin and Maxwell came from poverty. I wonder if that is the secret? Putin in St Petersburg, Maxwell in the village of Solotvyno now part of Ukraine where his father was a farm labourer. Perhaps when you have little, and you suffer and see those you love suffer, you are filled with the determination that it will not happen to you. But then many people are born into poverty who remain in poverty or who improve their lives without feeling the need to take over the world. I'm reminded of the story 'Love of Life' by Jack London in which a starving man is rescued by a ship. Soon after, wondering why the man is growing fat, the crew discover a store of biscuits under the man's bunk. Having been starving he was storing food unless the same thing happened to him again. I wonder if Maxwell, the poor boy set out to store money—other folk's money, lest he should become poor again. He wasn't a strong swimmer, evidently.

40.

Chilly. Grey above.

Amid what many see as the mash of mediocrity and moral paucity of the present administration in Britain, it's tempting as it always is, in moments when one's faith in the human race is threatened, to look back to sunnier times. To times when the Tory Party of Great Britain was represented by men of substance, of seriousness, of integrity. Men who put their country first and who were in essence decent. They wore smart suits, and their words were measured and seemingly well balanced. I'm looking back now to the 1950's and early sixties when Harold McMillan was Prime Minister. Yes, he was an Eton boy and a Balliol student (remind you of anyone?) whose studies were interrupted by the First World

War in which he was injured. He studied Latin and Greek, but he supported The Welfare State and strong Trade Unions in a mixed economy where some industries were nationalised. I saw him in the flesh once at The Usher Hall in Edinburgh when I was still at school. It was a memorable day and I was conscious of being in the presence of an impressive man. For PM = impressive. Despite his boast that we had 'never had it so good' his government fell after the Profumo affair and a decline in the balance of payments. The image of this man it has seemed to me recently symbolised a different kind of Conservative, but of course, in fact he was a Conservative in a different age.

He wasn't followed everywhere by cameras. Presumably he wasn't pestered by spin-doctors or policy groups. His was a pre-media-technology age when the gap between Power and People was greater. When we see Corn-mop sweating away his flab on his morning run or knocking down a Styrofoam brick wall in a bulldozer, we see the man in a way the public would never have seen Harold McMillan. Margaret Thatcher in her tank with goggles and a Union flag was a stage along the evolution of Statesman to celebrity politician: the invention of the photo-opportunity. But whether today's scrutiny is beneficial to our appreciation of our leaders is another matter.

A more recent nexus between the patrician Statesman and the man of straw comes in the shape of Alan Clark. I watched a film of the suave Mr Clark who was minister of State for Defence Procurement between 1989 and

1992. A self-confessed 'ladies' man', he climbed the greasy pole of Government appointments under Mrs. Thatcher until his attempt to undermine Government opposition to the sale of arms to Iraq led him to court for advising a firm on how to get round the embargo. Once in court he changed his account from his written evidence and when accused of lying, in a gem of political doublespeak said in the interview that he had been 'economic with the actualité.

' You'd spend a long time thinking that one up as another way of saying 'I lied' without using the word 'lied' but he managed it. I suppose a soupcon of

French helps to impart a little erudition—a bit of linguistic squid ink, to facilitate escape if you're too stupid to see through it, but his evasion does remind one of a certain Boris Johnson's apologists and evasions over the Party-gate scandals.

'I have no recollection' is a very useful exit from any guilt, as The Duke of York observed when presented with the photograph of him with his arm round Virginia Guiffre. When people say 'I have no recollection' why do they imagine that is enough to excuse them from whatever they are being accused of? It's not their memory that's on trial—it's their veracity. Presumably if Hitler had been put in the dock at Nuremberg he would have said 'I have no recollection of gassing Jewish people.' Well, that's fine Adolf. Off you go. The problem with telling lies when the evidence against you is overwhelming is that no-one believes you, but then that doesn't matter to most politicians. It didn't matter to Alan Clark. It doesn't matter to Boris Johnson, nor does it matter to his apologists.

Another classic from the 'Liars Playbook' is 'Let's move on.' We have a job to do and we must be getting on with it, so no distractions please such as accusing us of lying. Johnson's present 'distraction' comes at an appropriate time for him. Our modern Churchill has a war to fight over Putin's invasion of Ukraine. Well, not exactly a war to fight but a proxy war where we send weapons for others to use and fight. Looking back, perhaps the rot set in with the Profumo scandal and moved on through Thatcher and Jeremy Thorpe and David Cameron to where we are presently. At some stage in British politics a cynical disregard for truth moved into the house and the lodger has ensconced himself. MacMillan came from some of the same stables as Boris Johnson (Eton and Balliol), but he had a regard for people that this Neoliberal crew have lost. I believe we've never had it so bad.

41.

It's become cold. A damp grey chill that seeps into the bones in a way that blue-sky cold does not. It's a creepy, grey-sky cold that takes you. It's like a lie that settles and disturbs because there are no more clothes to put on to protect you from it. It's Britain today where our PM has broken the law.

If we ever doubted that politics has become the playground of the rich and the morally bankrupt, then today is proof. He was 'in attendance' at parties in Downing Street and they were parties not 'work gatherings.' Putin has not 'invaded' Ukraine-- his troops are involved in a 'military operation.' The fun in all this is listening to Corn-mop's apologists grasping for the evasions from The Playbook when most people know the truth. 'Now isn't the time to change a PM for we're in the middle of a war.' I didn't know that. Perhaps I've missed the planes overhead and the bombs dropping in Perthshire. Silly me. Oh, you mean Ukraine? Oh, right, and how are we fighting this war? We're helping. Weapons. Anti-tank grenade launchers. Armoured cars. Hundreds of them. That must cost a bit eh? That must cost quite a lot while poverty stalks Sunak-land. Not that we would resent helping Ukraine, but you wonder if that money is available for weapons why wasn't that money available before the war to help the poor? Oh, what a lovely war, for some people.

Just a couple of days ago we saw Corn-mop striding through Kyiv as the saviour of Ukraine. It makes a change from hunkering down in Downing Street with his spin-doctors wondering how he was going to wriggle free from the Party-gate scandal. 'We'll make you a war leader Boris. You've always wanted to be a Churchillian figure and now's your chance. Look, here's your ticket to Ukraine. No, there's no danger. The war's moved to the East. You can show how brave you are by being only a few hundred miles from the nearest Russian. They're making fatigues for you now. Carrie's just sewing a few Ukrainian badges on upstairs. Bound to go down well with that Zelenskyy chap…'

Then in steps the wisest spin-doctor. 'I'm just playing with an idea Boris. I wonder if fatigues might just be a step too far. I'm hearing "Oh look at Boris in his camouflage gear and he's nowhere near the fighting…" Get it? Just a tad obvious maybe. Why not a nice suit? The statesman. You're not posing as a member of Ukraine's army, you're here as the Prime Minister of Great Britain. They're not all stupid, unfortunately. Obvious isn't a good look. See what I'm getting at?'

Cunning prevails and Carrie stops work. Madame Defarge lays down her needle and thread as instructed though she is most unhappy and asks who it was who suggested a suit? Right. I've marked his card. Oh, and Rishi phoned. He's going to resign. God, what a wanker.'

'No, now isn't the time, Rishi. Are you serious Rishi? Can we just dump this moralising nonsense. This is politics Rishi. Now isn't the time to offer your resignation. If you go it'll put more pressure on me. We're in this together, right? Ever heard of loyalty? No, you won't ever be PM but come on, you haven't got what it takes man. Can't imagine you surviving the Commons these last few months. You know how you weep at films. Well, you can't do that at the dispatch box. Fucking pricks would smell your fear and pounce. Resilience Rishi. That's what I've got, and you don't. Oh, and you're too small and skinny to be a PM. So just fuck off back next door and see how much dosh the missus has made today.'

The grey cold seeps. The daffies are full of regret. Spring? Call this Spring?

42.

A Letter to Boris.

Today as I was brushing my teeth I hit upon an idea of entrepreneurial brilliance if I do say so myself. I will write to Boris Johnson and ask him to send me a piece of his ear-wax which I will then auction to Tory voters for a profit which will be distributed to the local party machine. Though wax may not vie with a heart or an ear or a finger in the list of the most wished-for relic of the saintly Boris, it is the least intrusive in not requiring him to suffer pain or demise. Baptized into the Roman Catholic Church as the faith of his mother, his conversion to The Anglican Church can only be regarded, as most decisions in Boris's life are now regarded, as a quixotic act of the moment rather than a spiritual transformation. I'm certain some vestigial Catholic impulse would incline Boris to believe that his earwax is of some spiritual value if not in Wigan then certainly in Richmond on Thames. I shall in my letter lay on thick my intense love of The Conservative Party and my deep appreciation for all that our dear Boris has done for the country.

Without his fast and effective action during the pandemic we would have lost more than the 160,000 who died in this country. Our vaccination programme saved countless lives while our European cousins were counting their innumerable dead and now he continues to prove himself as a leader in wartime by providing the small Ukrainian army with the necessary arms to defeat the might of Russia. I shall tell him how proud I felt to see him strolling through Kyiv with little Zelenskyy when most leaders of other countries were too afraid to visit. When I assure him that any funds engendered by the auction of his wax will be passed to my local Food Bank, I can only imagine the delight he might feel. I do hope however that dear Carrie will be close as the operation proceeds lest anything unfortunate happen and an eardrum be pierced. I couldn't forgive myself if such a thing were to occur. The letter will of course be private. I will not allow the great man's gift should I receive it, to be used by any devious politician as an indication of Boris's sense of sainthood. Modest as he is, I know how hurtful that would be.

43.

The sight of Priti Patel shaking hands over her arrangement to provide one-way tickets for 'illegal immigrants' to alight in Kigali cannot fail to swell the heart with pride. What other country, apart from Israel, Australia and allegedly Denmark (disappointing one that)) has the imagination to solve the influx of refugees from Iraq, Iran, Syria and more, by offering them a new beginning in other places? I imagine a government communication might go like this...

'We'd like to welcome you to Great Britain after your naughty little boat trip across the channel.

Unfortunately, we can't. You see you have come here illegally. You were not provided with a passport nor were you any part of our generous resettlement scheme to help those fleeing from war, famine or political oppression. You just thought you could take advantage of our humanity and paddle your rubber dinghy on to the beach and become British. Well, we have a plan for you. No, we're not going to send you back to France because these nasties that took money to get you here in the first place will be waiting for a second try. No, we're not going to put you up in a hotel for a few months while we work out exactly who you are and where you came from. We can't afford it. What we've decided to do for your best interests is to fly you to a place called Rwanda. You may not have heard of this country, but rest assured the few troubles it had in 1994 are forgotten now. It's a nice hilly country in the middle of Africa and its president is a nice man called Paul Kigame. Now we don't know what vicious rumours there are about Paul's regime, but as in most countries there are people who are always making up stories about how the President tries to eliminate his political opponents. Ignore these; just settle into your basic but very clean accommodation and make friends with some of the other refugees who have come here from places like Denmark and Israel. Some of them haven't made much effort to integrate and you might find them living destitute on the streets. Don't listen to their stories. They're just bitter about being refugees. If you like it in Kigali, you will get a nice job and you'll quickly realise how your life has changed for the better.

Yes, it's true that most people living there don't earn much but there is plenty of fresh food such as potatoes and bananas and crushed casava leaves to keep body and soul together and the weather is lovely. You'll probably feel at home with the weather considering where you came from which was probably quite hot.

Well as you can imagine, there isn't much more to communicate except that we have enjoyed having you for a brief time and though you broke the law coming here, Mrs. Patel doesn't hold grudges. She has a very difficult job to do and as the daughter of immigrants from Africa herself, she still has fond associations with Uganda which is not too far away from Rwanda.

Enjoy your trip and if you know of any other refugees that might like to join you it would be helpful if you could indicate a more direct route to Rwanda rather than through the UK. Oh, a final word: I hope you don't resort to the Law to appeal any extradition procedure. Involving the judiciary, who may just find ways to uphold your appeal will only exacerbate the situation. Just think of what it would look like if a plane capable of carrying two hundred people ended up leaving with only a handful, or even… No. Have faith in the Government's plans for you and bear in mind this is the only way to end the traffickers wicked schemes.'

44.

The obliteration of Ukraine is slipping down the

news headlines: more important that we're packing

off refugees to Rwanda,(that oasis of peace and

humanity in the heart of Africa,) film of mudslides in

Kwa Zulu Natal or the death of a pop drummer

through a drugs overdose; why even the belief by Michael Fabricant, he of the very odd hair, that teachers often had a drink in the classroom after a stressful day, in mitigation of Corn-mop's misadventures in No 10. We are so inured to Corn-mop's apologists and their puerile inventions that they really are beyond discussion, but that doesn't stop the BBC. Sometimes 'balance' (in the studio on my right is Mr Reason and on my left Mr Totally Silly) brings out the most extraordinary toads from under their stones. Meanwhile the people of Ukraine suffer the daily bombardment by Russian missiles: old women crouch in damp cellars with buckets for toilets, in their eyes a dull bewilderment that such things could happen again. And what do we do in the cosy West? We watch the missiles strike and unhook ourselves from guilt by providing arms. If there is one lesson to be learned among the many, it is that a group of nations with their own interests is ill-equipped to deal with one nation whose interests are clear. We saw the tanks gathering for weeks. We believed it was an 'exercise' because we were told so and we desperately wanted to believe it. We had no answer for an invasion. Now we are relieved that Ukraine is not a member of NATO for we are not obliged to fight with her. We fear Putin's threats of nuclear war. One wonders what Putin will think if, and when, he annexes the Donbas region. A job if not completely successful, successful enough in that it has shown how threats of nuclear war can frighten The West. Now for the Baltic, with threats made already to Finland and Sweden should they join NATO.

While The West's response has been mainly economic in terms of sanctions and the seizure of

Oligarch assets, Germany's reluctance to end its reliance on Russian gas and oil still provides the Russian coffers with $700 million a day. And yet it's not difficult to see Germany's problem. 55% of her gas comes from Russia and 34% of her oil. Economists in Germany have warned of the dire financial consequences of suddenly cutting off these supplies. The German government, aware of the pressures, has promised to cut supplies as soon as possible and fully within two years. Meanwhile Russia accepts her payments in Euros which Gazprom converts to Rubles. Germany's interests are best served by stabilizing her economy and somehow ending her reliance on fossil fuels from Russia. Criticism by other European countries that are not reliant on Russian fuel is understandable but not realistic.

After considerable opposition within Germany, she has now given permission to other countries to send their German made weapons to Ukraine and is herself sending weapons. But as Russian forces mass on the Eastern border to invade The Donbas, Ukraine's forces outmanned it is estimated 5 to 1, it's unlikely that they will be able to hold their positions weapons or no weapons. Biden offers money and weapons. We all offer weapons and refuge for those fleeing Russian incursions, but surely the bottom line is simple—does Russia make gains from this conflict? As I suggested before, if the Donbas is won and annexed as a part of Russia, Putin has won. His loss of men and materiel has been worth it. Chechnya, The Crimea, The Donbas. Bit by bit he extends his territory on the pretext of keeping NATO at bay. If Finland and Sweden join NATO then will he feel threatened in the Baltic? We are tired of assertions that NATO is a Treaty organization, a defensive Bloc, not an offensive one, but Putin either doesn't believe this or pretends not to believe it in his quest to re-establish the old USSR. What can The West do now? What have we learned from this?

The West have for years been blind to the sort of man they are dealing with. London has thrived on the money-laundering of Russian oligarchs who stole from their own people. The Tory party has accepted donations and watched as these men have amassed their wealth. They are complicit in his crimes. But then so are we all who have stood by and watched The Crimea being taken, Chechen being taken. We have seen how any demonstration against the regime has been stamped out; just how authoritarian the Russian government have become as they censor the

Press and send their operatives abroad to silence their critics. Was Salisbury and Litvinenko poisoning not an indication of the sort of people we were dealing with? We made a fuss, but the oligarchs remained. Now we have woken up. The whole of Europe has woken up to possibilities but how united are we in standing up to him? Other countries are now vulnerable to the dreams of a callous man and one who is now on the way to being officially classified a 'war-criminal.'

Vladimir Putin was born and raised in Leningrad; a city besieged by the Germans within living memory. Every year on 29th January he lays a wreath to commemorate the ending of the siege of his city by the Nazis, a siege in which his own father was wounded. Now Putin's soldiers have laid siege to Mariupol where, as in Leningrad, people take refuge in cellars. Putin has a warped understanding of history. He has turned the besiegers into heroes and the besieged into Nazis*. There was only one way to defeat Hitler's Nazis and that was to defeat them by arms. Arms are needed again, but this time The West must not have one tied behind its back.

* It hasn't gone unnoticed that The Azov Regiment, the one besieged in the Steelworks in Mariupol does seem to be made up of Far-right extremists who sport Nazi emblems. This does in no way validate Putin's claim that the Ukraine is full of Nazis but does beg the question as to why this group are an accepted part of the Ukrainian armed forces.

45.

Chilly. Grey above.

The present invasion of Ukraine and the callous

treatment of the indigenous citizens by Russian

soldiers is a chilling reminder of the same treatment

perpetrated on the German population in 1945 as Stalin's forces made their victorious way to Berlin. What had occurred in Leningrad and before had deeply scarred the Russian psyche and the hatred felt for the invading Nazis and their crimes was no doubt the driving force behind Russian revenge against the German civilian population. Present atrocities perpetrated by the Russian army against Russian speaking people have no such equivalent psychological impetus and can only be explained by ill-discipline and a failure of command. The brutality shown in Chechnya and in Syria now seems to be a part of the Russian War Playbook. Summary execution, rape, and disregard for the distinction between soldier and civilian or between civilian and military infrastructure makes Putin's war the war of a criminal mind with no regard for international conventions. Designating him 'a war criminal' may appease our disgust, but it's difficult to see this criminal ever being brought to justice. The West has come to realise the depth of hatred and mistrust this man has for the democracies of Western Europe and the USA—a hatred fuelled by the collapse of the USSR under Gorbachev whose reforms encouraged a move towards complete self-government in many of the old Soviet Republics who were until then part of a Federation of autonomous states. The brief flirtation with 'democracy' by reforms in the eighties through Brezhnev and Gorbachev's perestroika and glasnost led to a desire for ethnic identity and the resultant de-colonisation that ultimately caused the dissolution of the USSR. When Yeltsin became head of state in 1991 he dissolved the Russian Congress and created a super-presidential constitution which paved the way for his successor Vladimir Putin. Yeltsin's attempts to modernize Russia did not include dissolving the KGB which in hindsight may have been a mistake. Putin, as an ex-KGB officer no doubt brought this mindset to his office as President. But through all this there remains a question: why do the Russian people, offered a taste of democracy in the eighties and nineties when their failing command economy could have been turned into a free market one, end up with the oligarchic theft of its mineral assets and the resultant assumption of a new Tsar in the shape of Vladimir Putin? Perhaps acceptance of the autocratic rule of 'Tsars' whether born in palaces or from the streets of Leningrad is so deeply a part of the Russian psyche from the time of Nicholas 1 till the Revolution of 1917 that the flirtations with change in the latter years of the twentieth century were doomed to failure. As Colin Thubron discovers in his book of travels 'Among the Russians' there was in the eighties a nostalgic fondness for Stalin from many in Khrushchev's Russia. The recurring epithet, heard today when autocratic leaders are discussed, is 'strong.' Never mind the hundreds of thousands who were killed—Stalin was 'a strong leader.' Putin is no doubt considered by many in Russia as a 'strong leader' which must mean he tolerates no opposition. What, one wonders is the psychology of a people who need this kind of strength to lead them? And to what are they being led? Donald Trump, a great admirer of Putin as a 'strong leader' harboured similar feeling towards those who disagreed with him, amply demonstrated during his election campaign and subsequently by his treatment of the Press. Perhaps the fondness, or rather need for a strong leader comes from a deep insecurity in the populace; from the dehumanisation of the individual whose every impulse becomes subsumed by the dictats of the State.

Masha Gessen's book 'The Future of History' subtitled 'How Totalitarianism reclaimed Russia' attempts through focusing on the lives of a group of seven people, to untangle the mind-set of what is described as 'Homo-Sovieticus.' Though her group are not representative of Russian society as a whole, their personal accounts reveal how the return to autocracy since the Presidency of Vladimir Putin has affected their lives. Only one of the group, Alexander Dugin was a supporter of Putin and his invention of a political philosophy based on the notion of 'The Russian World' seeks to disengage Russia from The

West and its democratic toxins and provides an intellectual basis for Putin's actions.

Gessen uses an anecdote to illustrate the Russian mind. One of a group after waiting for an hour for a metro ticket, buys a bunch of them and offers them free to those still queueing. He is arrested, though he has broken no laws other than breaking the mould of accepted behaviour and thinking outside the box—he was organising rather than being organised. Gessen also makes an important point when he/she says that 'scarcity is essential for the survival of totalitarian regimes.' While some gesture of punishment is necessary for the illegal invasion of Ukraine, he/she doesn't believe that a people struggling to survive is enough to topple an autocratic leader. One must suppose that it's the sense of all being in this together and the attribution of their troubles to some external enemy that justifies this belief. Gessen believes that sanctions have never succeeded in bringing down a regime. One supposes it depends on who the people blame for their struggles—the countries imposing sanctions or their leader. If the propaganda machine at work in The Kremlin continues to 'work' it seems unlikely that Russians will turn against Putin, for Putin's story is the only one they will hear.

A story on the radio this morning of a woman living in the North of Ukraine whose brother lives five miles away over the border in Belorussia. She will never speak to him again she says, for he supports what Putin is doing. Of course he does—not because he's Russian but because he 'voted' for Putin, and he listens to Putin. He'd probably have refused the free ticket in case the KGB were watching.

46.

A Low is over us. Grey skies and drizzle.

The future looks frightening. It's difficult to see a resolution of the Ukraine conflict without escalation. I suspect Russia will not tolerate weapons being ushered into Ukraine for much longer. If the threat of nuclear conflict is made, how can The West back down? And the threat once made can always be made. Can we really witness the complete annihilation of the major cities of Europe and America? No. For we'll all be dead as radiation sweeps across the world. How can China and India stay silent as Putin threatens life on Earth? Radiation doesn't stop at borders.

Scandals proliferate involving the Tory party. One Tory MP was spotted watching porn on his phone in The House of Commons chamber by two women of his own party. After a delay of a few days, he has resigned his seat.

This following the accusation from some Tory MP's that Angela Rayner sitting on Labour's Front Bench crosses and uncrosses her legs a la Basic Instinct's Sharon Stone in order to distract Boris Johnson. What does she do now—cross them more blatantly or wear trousers?

Local Government elections On Thursday 5th May will be a test of whether the English electorate are as sensitive to the Tory Party's shot feet as non-Tory voters. Here in Scotland the denial by Labour, The Conservative party and the Liberal party of what a vast number of Scots wish, will see them slaughtered again at the polls.

47. It's the Law, folks.

Reading in The Guardian today about a Police 'initiative' in England invented by Margaret Thatcher called 'Secured by Design.' This in effect gives police forces the right to determine whether the street furniture or topography of a public space may contribute towards the incidence of anti-social behaviour. The removal of benches from parks, is justified by the police as an attempt to deter anti-social conduct which is deemed to occur on them or near them. This, together with the new laws governing Protest is a glaring example of the trap which governments fall into when laws proliferate. The French 17th century philosopher Montaigne wrote, 'The most desirable laws are those which are fewest, simplest and most general.' He railed against laws which tried to catch up with every minor human transgression, making the point that 'There is hardly any relation between our actions (which are always changing) and fixed unchanging laws.' An example might be Putin's Russia where opposition to the action in Ukraine will require as many laws to arrest it as there are ways to object to the 'war.' You may be arrested for holding a blank sheet of A4 above your head. Obviously, you've just forgotten to write 'No War' on it, but the police get the message. During the Covid pandemic, attempts to prevent spread occasioned so many 'laws' that the public became confused as to what was legal and what not. Cornmop himself seemed either puzzled by this or didn't give a toss. Luckily, he's received his comeuppance which in quieter and more moral times would have led to his resignation. He must be a secret supporter of Glasgow Rangers supporters whose motto during their financial shenanigans was 'We don't do walking away.' As a hero of the Ukraine's fighting forces for his weapons contributions, he clings on, but the smell of his indiscretions pervades every aspect of Westminster politics.

What strikes one reading Montaigne or the Greek philosophers today is how germane their words still are in relation to human conduct. While Montaigne quotes Epicurus, who wrote '…we were once distressed by crimes, now by laws' Montaigne's agreement with these words seventeen hundred or more years later, indicates how rational thought spans the ages.

48.

Blustery day with grey skies.

Blustery days for Keir Starmer who has risked his political future on the findings by Durham police regarding his 'party.'
In today's Guardian an article suggesting it's a tit-for-tat situation from which we should all move on. Well,

it's not. Corn-mop lied to the House of Commons, and it has yet to be proved whether Starmer has lied about his 'party.' He has never denied that he was in a room where some of his electioneering colleagues were eating their take-away curries and having a beer and maintains that he has broken no rules. The point is not the parties but the lying. Starmer may not be a very charismatic politician (an understatement, probably) but he seems a decent man and has put his integrity before his ambitions to be Prime Minister. If he does go, it is doubly sad that the charismatic Rayner will go with him. Now there's a lady who could have touched parts of England that Starmer will never reach. She's a lager-lass.

Northern Ireland has found its future and it lies not with the DUP, that august party of loyal neanderthals clinging to their royalist Protestant roots in an Island of Catholic conspiracy, but to Sinn Fein, ('we ourselves') a party dedicated to re-unification. The Alliance Party took votes from the DUP allowing SF in through the back door. The poor old DUP has been thoroughly dup-ed by Corn-mop who promised there would be no barrier between Great Britain and Northern Ireland. He told them that "no British government could or should" sign up to putting a border in the Irish Sea between mainland United Kingdom and Northern Ireland. Less than one year later there was a border. Now that's classic Corn-mop, a man who sees no link between a promise and its fulfilment. Life's a fucking joke, ain't it. Well, the gentlemen and ladies of the DUP have decided that unless the Protocol is torn up, they won't be taking their seats in that monstrous effigy to powerlessness—Stormont. What about the folk who voted for them? Empty seats in Stormont?

Talking of Stormont, that grandiose pile on a hill with its half-mile drive, reminds me of Putin's 'victory' parade yesterday. Both seem to suggest power but in reality, are symbols of insecurity. Style but no substance. Ranks of goose-stepping soldiers and a parade of military hardware are presumably intended to make us fear the might of Russia, just as the intimidating frontage of Stormont is intended to impress us with the seriousness of Northern Ireland as a state. Do the strong need to show us how strong they are, or does their strength lie in knowing that strength does not require to be exhibited? As Russian troops struggle in the Donbas, Putin has nothing to boast. His grand plan for Ukraine is in tatters and it can't be long before he either goes for broke with some unforeseen escalation or accepts a peace deal that only he would claim to be a victory. Ukraine will not give up any territory. What will Putin do when his troops are bogged down in an interminable war while The West pours new and more effective weapons into Ukraine?

A survey undertaken by the banned newspaper Novaya Gazeta has found that people under thirty in Russia are much more likely to have feelings of disquiet or opposition to the war than those over sixty. Perhaps they want a future. I suppose access to social media where that is possible may be the reason for this. Unfortunately, protest is dangerous and therefore the Kremlin media machine continues to grind out its version of the 'military operation.' A clip on TV yesterday of Russian bodies being collected and bagged by Ukrainian soldiers made me wonder if the ill-discipline of Russian troops extends to leaving their dead on the battlefield. I do fervently hope that this was not a propaganda exercise by the Ukrainians and that the bodies in the black bags were in fact Russian and not Ukrainian. Surely all armies recover their dead.

49.

A day of rain and gray skies. Everything droops. Apart from Classic FM.

Listening to this station this morning I became conscious of how irritating Alexander Armstrong's voice is. Nice guy, but it's the ineluctable jollity that wears you down. I mean Classic thingy is bad enough in its endless repetition of the words 'relax' and 'smooth' but when you add Armstrong's ineffable jolliness it creeps into unlistenable territory. I ditched jollity years ago when life started kicking in or should I say when life began to give me a good kicking. I wonder sometimes what demographic CFM is aimed at. The choice of music is a bit Prince Charles rather than avant-garde in its fixation with 'easy-listening' Mozart and Vivaldi as if twentieth or twenty-first century music doesn't exist. Bartok, Shostakovich, oh the list would be endless if I knew the names, but for your average CFM listener it's all 'music to relax to' and very 'smooth. 'I'm studying for my A-levels and I'd like some nice soothing music to relieve my anxiety. I've had a wank but that didn't do it.' Well, how about a nice bit of Mozart? And even more irritating are the league tables such as 'top one hundred' or 'top fifty' or 'top ten.' This is top of the pops country for old Mozart and Antonio—the Beatles and the Elvises of CFM. Does everything have to be a competition before it's of any interest? The whole business speaks of patronising the plebs who think they're a cut above because they know that Mozart's dead and they recognise Eine Kline Nachtmusik.

Speaking of Prince Charlie, he seemed rather ill at ease as he delivered his mum's Speech to Parliament. There he was sitting on the Regent's seat—can't sit on Queenie's seat— and next to him on a velvet cushion was the crown which I thought was very tough on a man who's been waiting to put that hat on for so many years. No wonder he couldn't really concentrate as he read out Corn-mop's repressive measures on the velum. Another aspect of our wonderful Royal family is the number of medals the male members sport on these occasions. It makes your average Queen's Scout look as if he's only done his campfire badge. This is 2022 and still we bow and scrape before this intellectually limited family whose only achievements are being who they are and driving helicopters or as a hobby, whipping horses on their horse-drawn carriages.

But hey, it's the Queen's Jubilee folks. Three thousand years on the throne is something for the plebs to get excited about isn't it. We'll get the usual English crowds down The Mall waving their Union

Jacks and wetting themselves that one of the Royals waved at them: 'No, really, he looked right at me and waved. It's the most wonderful moment of my life, apart from when my cat didn't die of course.' Watching the Queen's Speech with the nonsense that goes with it—the whole historical dressing-up box raided, the wigs, the men's tights, the woman (who says we're old-fashioned!) banging her black rod against the door to get in: all so traditional and stuck in memories of the long past that you either embrace as a charming indication of stability (and yes, ritual has a function in our lives), or as many do, an indication that the twenty-first century hasn't touched this sceptred Isle. Parliament itself is as anachronistic as the clothes these folk were wearing: a chamber that can't seat all its members and one with benches upholstered in green leather, the discomfort no doubt intended to keep members awake. No desks of course and no computers within a mile, so you queue to go through the lobby to vote. I've written this before and I make no apology for it. When will things change and let the daylight of contemporary times in? It's an antiquated chamber where adversarial politics is played out, each side braying against the other. Is it any wonder that we're in this political mess?

No Party that wins an election seems willing to affect change in our antiquated voting system. FPTP is anti-democratic in terms of votes cast and acts against a government of the best minds which a coalition might just give us. We stagger from term to term with no prospect of long-term planning.

50.

Warming up. Sun again.

As London swelters, on the National News we are kept abreast of developments in the Rooney versus Vardy defamation case. Two 'wags' as the term has it, spatting it out in the High Court at great expense. Hey. We're footballer's wives don't you know, and money ain't an issue. Does it not say something about our society that the men and women behind BBC News imagine that this item is of more interest to the Great British Public than the men and women dying in

Ukraine? Oh, and Corn-mop won't be getting any more FPN's. One up for him while Starmer sweats over whether his integrity will lead him into political exile. If Starmer thinks his resignation would be followed by that of Corn-mop, then he's on another universe. Corn-mop reminds me of a worm that once pierced, wriggles off the hook, falls onto the grass and wounded, wriggles away to fuck itself and have children. Well, he wriggled off the Covid hook that was an oxygen mask and all to end up at home breaking his own rules, clever little worm that he is.

David Blunkett, or Lord Blunkett as he now is, was on TV's Politics Today. As he spoke, I was reminded of a previous thought; that the politicians of yesterday were men of some calibre. He is thoughtful, respectful, loves his dog and has an air of confidence in what he says that puts the present lot to shame.

You don't get the feeling as he is speaking that he is speaking to an agenda but rather he is telling the truth as he sees it. One wonders if in this age of mass media where everyone and their dog has an opinion and can express it, even me, and where many opinions are potently vile and harmful, we will ever regain a political and social landscape that isn't littered with lies and half-truths. It's easy for spreaders of lies and half-truths to influence the supremely stupid or those millions supremely angry that the world hasn't given them what they deserve. It's also possible to demolish truth a la Trump and just call anything he doesn't like 'fake news.' Suspicion and a widespread belief in conspiracy theories is fertile ground for the Right as has been proved in America where the GOP has turned into a neo-fascist cabal.

If there's one thing that can support right-wing conspiracy theories, it's that old walking stick that the morbidly brain-lame rely on in times of doubt— what does The Bible say? Well, you don't have to read the bible to suspect that God doesn't do abortion, or Black People or Homosexuals and if God doesn't like them neither should you. Apart from Billy Graham, America's TV evangelists are a shoddy bunch of fear mongers and anger stirrers who know how to make a quick buck. They make snake-oil purveyors seem like quite nice folk.

But the gullibility of large swathes of America's good God-fearing people enables a plethora of 'preachers' to fleece these poor souls of their cash in order to get closer to God. Jim Bakker and his first wife, Jimmy Swaggart, Martin Gorman, Jesse Duplantis and Robert Tilton all have two things in common—they are tele-evangelists, and they are all alleged con-men who allegedly use the Bible to extort money from their listeners. The fact that some have been convicted and yet return to the airwaves says it all. If you fear God and you listen to this lot, you are at risk of being duped. And if you believe anything Donald Trump says you are also being duped. I suspect it's the same people being duped, don't you? Trouble is, there are about seventy million of them. We live in the age of the dupe.

I began writing this with the conviction that the world was going to hell on a hand cart because daily I see news on TV of war, of internecine conflict, of mothers murdering their children, of women being murdered and raped, of politicians and their sleezy obfuscations. Good news?

There was little good news around today apart from a man wounded in the Manchester bombing who is ascending Kilimanjaro in his wheelchair. Well, he's being pulled up Kilimanjaro, but he is helping to propel himself. if he hadn't been wounded that wouldn't be news, but a closer look at the reality of what is happening in the world when we compare today with last century or the century before that, shows that poverty has decreased, literacy has increased, and fewer people go hungry. There has however been a drop in the last two years of the number of people living in a democracy. According to the Economic Intelligence Unit 47% of the world's population now live in democracies of one type or another which means that vast numbers of people live in autocracies or dictatorships. Why? That's for another day.

51.

A grey day. Cool.

I'm thinking today about 'The Nanny State.' That's the one which makes laws supposedly removing the choices you might make regarding the conduct of your everyday life. That's the State that made it the law to wear a seatbelt for the statistics proved that you're twice as likely to die in an accident if you are not wearing a seatbelt. We've been forced to become safer. Still 7% of drivers don't wear seat belts. Presumably they either feel invulnerable or have political objections to The Nanny State telling them what to do, so they'll risk shooting through a windscreen or a steering wheel punching a hole in their chests. Their choice.

The Nanny State's bans on Cigarette advertising, and the ban in 2006 on smoking in public spaces such as bars and restaurants and later in cars with children have led to a reduction in lung-cancer deaths. A Glasgow University study showed that, before the smoking ban, the number of hospital admissions of children with asthma was increasing on average by five per cent each year in Scotland. In the three years after the ban, admissions decreased 18 per cent per year. In the three months after the ban there was a 6.3 per cent drop in the volume of cigarettes sold in England. Two examples of the effect on the population of state intervention and yet there is at the heart of The Conservative Party strong opposition to such measures exemplified by the very invention of the pejorative term 'Nanny State.' Just this week another area of concern for the medical profession—the 'obesity crisis' has hit the headlines.

Plans for the NHS to intervene have however been stymied.

A proposed Bill drawn up by the Government to ban junk-food advertising and multi-buy supermarket deals has been postponed. I use the word 'postponed' but some even more cynical might use another expression such as 'kicked into the long grass from which it will never be found again.' Childhood obesity and the fact that two out of three of the adult population is overweight was highlighted during the Covid crisis where obesity was cited as a major cause of Covid deaths.

It is impossible to exist in our society without being bombarded by food adverts and for many it's impossible to resist their allure. Signs on take-away outlets saying 'don't cook, just eat' are intended to boost fast-food take-aways that have now become such a part of our daily lives. Company's such as 'Deliveroo' are thriving on the delivery of fast food to our door and in a busy world where many acknowledge the convenience of not having to cook a meal, the poor nutritional value of many of these meals is conducive to obesity as is the proliferation of 'deals' on food with poor nutritional value. As a society we have become addicted to salt and fat and sugar but there is a more sinister aspect to this problem and that is the direct correlation between income and diet.

The poorer you are the more likely you are to buy cheap food, and by definition 'budget food' is not quality food. Research in America showed clearly that obesity among the white population was most prevalent in

the poorest states such as Oklahoma,

Arkansas and Mississippi and less prevalent in

relatively wealthier states such as California

and the Northeastern states. In America in

addition to junk food, soft drinks made from

high fructose corn syrup are responsible for

much obesity. In this country just last week a

Tory minister in an interview in response to a

question about how poorer people could cope

with the cost-of-living crisis advised that

struggling families could save money by

buying 'budget' brands in their supermarket

shopping rather than proprietary ones.

What's the message there then? If you are

poor, you should just buy the cheapest food

you can afford. This, from the same playbook

as 'if you haven't enough money just ask for

a rise' from another Tory MP. Even if you ate

bad food but accepted that exercise would

help, if you're poor and putting on weight

you can't afford to join a gym. If you are

poor, you can't afford to eat in a nice

restaurant. Those areas where obesity levels

are greatest in England are the areas of greatest unemployment such as the Northeast. But all this aside, we wonder why the government has U-turned on a crucial plan.

Well, there is a war in Ukraine, the 'Bread-basket' of Europe, and prices are rising in our supermarkets. If the poor are to eat, they must be able to eat cheaply. Ergo— junk food must be available. That's the rationale from this Tory administration. Now just isn't a good time to attack obesity in our adults or children. Those are the words of

wisdom from Tory MP's whose meals are

subsidised in the House of Commons

restaurant where a main meal of steak costs

a mere £9. Jamie Oliver, that crusader over

the years for healthy school meals and better

food for all, is rightly appalled at the

Government's decision. Is it another case of

Tory opposition to The Nanny State? Is it a

case of 'if poor people want to become

obese, it's their choice?' I blame Marie

Antoinette for a lot of this food politics. Cake indeed.

As in every case of State intervention in matters of public safety and health one could argue that proven benefits to the population should not be left to choice on the part of the individual. Politics aside, surely if a state can legislate to increase the safety of its citizens, then that is a good thing. Seatbelt-wearing, smoking and obesity are all areas in which some degree of state control have been effected. The latter trails behind the other two in terms of legal measures to control it

but will offer society even more benefits

when it's addressed. Obesity is not just

harmful to those who suffer it; the results of

obesity include the costs of the diseases

exacerbated by it. The NHS, already

struggling with a backlog of serious cases

while Covid was the priority, needs all the

help it can get to avoid having to deal with

heart disease, diabetes, strokes,

osteoarthritis and high blood pressure, all of

which may be attributed to obesity. As in

other areas of reform however it's obvious that 'lobbying' by those with vested interests is at play.

The food companies who produce our processed foods high in fat and sugar must accept responsibility for this crisis. No-one argues against the addictive properties of these constituents, and once hooked it's difficult to change habits to eating foods with less of these ingredients. By 2040 it is estimated that 47 million Britons will be overweight—a staggering prediction of the near future and one that in present day terms would surely destroy our health system. A good State looks after its people and has a duty to keep them safe. Our people must eat more wisely, and they must be given the money to do so. The government knows this, and yet they are slow to implement measures to improve the situation. Why?

That the poor grow fat while the rich remain thin is one of the paradoxes of our time.

52.

Grey skies again with slight rain.

As children we learn and unlearn things about life. One of the things we unlearn if we are wise is that there is no such thing as 'fairness' in life. Fairness, if we strive for it in our understanding of the world will soon let us down. I write this as two footballers wives battle in the High court over whether one leaked details of the other's confidences to the Press. Now I've learned in life that sheep are stupid because they can afford to be. Little pressure is put upon a sheep to attain anything other than grass to make life worth living. Any sheep with a phenomenal brain would surely be shunned by the others as a show-off if it read a book in a shady corner of the field. Dogs have their enhanced ability to smell and other instincts that aid their self-preservation, but they can't speak or write novels or even change a light bulb because they have no need to do such things. Where am I going? I'm going in the direction of footballer's wives who in the same vein as sheep and dogs have no reason to be more intelligent than they are, for their instinct led

them to marry rich footballers and with the

hair and the make-up and the plumped lips

and the very large shades, they have

everything they need to be happy. Well,

you'd think so, but they also have Twitter,

and they use this to make others unhappy.

While the female Vardy's and Rooney's bask

in the spotlight of their bickering, there is a

war in Europe.

Old women and children huddle in damp

and dark basements with minimum water and

food while the clump of shelling can be heard above ground. Wives lose their husbands and children their fathers. Homes are destroyed, cities such as Mariupol razed. A wasteland is created of destruction and human misery while the footballer's wives return from court to their commodious dwellings no doubt feeling that life is tough. It's not fair some would say, and they'd be right in the sense that some suffer while others, might one even say others less talented, sleep in their silk sheets or drink their Prosecco. One could almost forgive them were they to show any indication that they were aware of the comfort of their little lives, but they don't. The rich get richer while the poorer visit the Food Bank.

While we're on the subject of Banks, I've concluded that the only good bank is the food bank. All the others are money-making machines who pay next to nothing for my cash which they invest and make whacking profits. As an ex-teacher the word 'bonus' was an alien concept to me, but it seems many bank workers receive bonuses for doing

what they're paid to do. Is that fair? No, it's

not, but I suppose if your organisation makes

a profit or you contribute to that profit, then

you are thanked by being given a BONUS.

Unfortunately, schools don't make money,

hospitals don't make money, fire-stations

don't make money and the police don't make

money, so if you're looking for a bonus,

people, you need to get out of the Public

Sector. Now is that fair? No. Oh, I forgot—if

you're a CEO running a hospital or a local

authority then you will get a bonus. Why?

Because you're worth it. It's the market rate

or something.

53. Blue sky. Fluffy clouds.

Mhairi Black the SNP Westminster MP, two days ago, appropriately attired in black and with an unashamedly Scottish proletarian accent waved a paper and warned the House of Commons that the 'F' word was becoming applicable to this government. Well, the usual 'F' word wouldn't be a shock but this one was 'Fascist.' Strong stuff, but perhaps not surprising given the mutual hatred between the Tory benches and those of the SNP. Other than another blast at the Government, is there any justification for her warning?

Madeleine Albright, the first woman to serve as American Secretary of State (1997-2001) who died this year, published a book 'Fascism—a Warning' in 2018. Living as she did through the Trump presidency, it's no coincidence that her mind was drawn to her subject. It's a collection of reminiscences and essays on some of the notable autocrats of recent years, many of whom she knew personally. On the inside jacket there is a quotation from Primo Levi who wrote that 'every age has its own fascism' and I suppose that's as true as saying every age has its own buildings or its own kinds of cars. But it's accurate in the sense that 'fascism' can elude an easy definition. It has become a general term of abuse directed at any person or political system that you despise without further justification being required. It's a muddy word that you hope will stick.

If we examine the word carefully, Benito Mussolini bursts into the room claiming ownership. Of Etruscan origin, the Romans used the *'fasces'* —a bundle of sticks (strength) around an axe (punishment?), carried by the Lictors to symbolise power. Mussolini, expelled from the Socialist Party, created his own Fascist Party in 1921. Anti-socialist, Nationalist and determined to stamp out opposition, it fed on dissatisfaction over the outcomes of the First World War for Italy. Whereas socialism was seen as an economic solution, fascism was now a

solution of Government.

Key elements in fascism as a political

movement are a powerful leader and an elite

(Putin/ Oligarchs); a powerful Nationalist

narrative; control of the media and

consequently of opposition, and control of

the Judiciary. If we return to Albright's book,

we see clearly elements of the fascist

Playbook in the form of Donald Trump. The

call to 'Make America Great Again,' the

narcissistic demeanour fuelled by a talent for

persuading gatherings that he was 'one of them' in his opposition to Washington—the enemy—you need one; his disdain for the Press in his use of the term 'fake news' to repel any criticism; his injunction to his supporters to throw out or in one case to beat up any hecklers at his meetings; his maneuvering to get right wing judges on the Supreme Court. Trump didn't kill anyone or was ever accused of having an opponent killed as is the case with many fascist dictators; he didn't expel artists and intellectuals either, but as can be easily demonstrated his direction of travel was along the fascist road. He was still learning. Orban, Erdogan, Lukashenko, Amin, Xi Jinping, Putin and many others have followed the fascist route—one so well-travelled that autocratic states resemble one another politically and socially. Why then did Black wave her paper and use the 'F' word?

Opposite her on the government benches she sees a front bench filled with public schoolboys, a Prime Minister educated at Eton and a Chancellor who is a multi-millionaire. She sees wealth and privilege running the country. Is Johnson a powerful leader? Well, put it this way, he has the power. Does he have an elite under him? Why yes. Not many working-class men and women in that cabinet. Is there a powerful Nationalist narrative? Well taking Britain out of the European Union was not done because we felt too humble to be a member. Brexit was about the notion that Britain, she of the once Empire, would be better off by herself rather than bound within a confederation of European States. 'Get Brexit Done' was a call to those who believed membership of the E.U. was detrimental to all that Britain could be when freed from E.U. regulations. Immigration was a key issue with many voters who were persuaded that 'free-movement' within the E.U. was adversely affecting the quality of life of British citizens. Now, if that's not a tilt towards nationalist feeling I don't know what is. That Brexit was good for Britain was inextricably linked with a belief that Britain outside the EU could be made

'great again.' If we'd lost some mythic

'greatness' (Great Britain) then with

deregulation, 'free-ports' and the whole

world to trade with, we would be rich and

powerful again. A strong leader, an elite, a

Nationalist narrative, well that's fine but far

short of fascism. What about the press and

the media?

With two exceptions—The Guardian and

The Daily Mirror, every newspaper in Britain

supported the Tory Party in the 2019 General

Election. Why? Because they are all owned by

billionaires with vested interests in a free-

market Neo-liberal economy favoured by The

Tory Party. The BBC, the National

Broadcaster has had its license fee frozen for

two years contributing to a funding crisis.

Many believe that the Tory party would

welcome the privatisation of this channel

which would inevitably challenge the

integrity of its neutral political stance. Any

sense that that neutrality could be challenged

is grist to the Government's mill. Channel 4 is

another public service broadcaster whose

charter is under review and in danger of

privatisation which will inevitably affect the

quality of programmes. Profit will be the

guiding principle. Surely the above list seems

to be stretching things too far in terms of

fascism. What about the judiciary?

Oh well I'm afraid that's going to be

another tick. In 2016 the high court ruled

that parliament and not the prime minister

by use of prerogative powers would need to

trigger Article 50 to start the UK's exit from

the European Union. The Daily Mail's front page pictured three judges with the headline 'Enemies of the People.' Later Boris Johnson attempted to prorogue parliament for five weeks in August 2019 and after the assent of the Queen (did she have an option?) it was left to the Supreme Court and Lady Hale to judge the ruling 'unlawful' much to the Tory Party's chagrin. Opposition parties would have had two weeks less to debate any anti no-deal legislation and one wonders if that could in any way have been behind the move.

Surely not. The Government and the judiciary: Trump and The Supreme Court. Those in power do not enjoy any obstacle to the exercise of their power whether they are fully paid-up members of the fascist club or perhaps like our Prime Minister and his government merely saving up to become members.

With a majority of eighty MP's the power lies in the hands of The Tory Party—a Party whose antics in Downing Street during lockdown have exposed serious questions regarding the integrity of Boris Johnson and more tellingly, the integrity of those who continue to support him. The Republican Party's devotion to Donald Trump in the face of his narcissistic hate-filled ramblings is a chilling reminder of what a jobs-worth mindset can do to a party. Oh, did I say 'party'? Silly me—it was a work gathering. Mhairi, we're not quite there yet, but good for you to notice the signs.

As for the Russian people, Arthur Miller touched on a fundamental issue when he wrote, "Few of us can easily surrender our belief that society must somehow make sense. The thought that the State has lost its mind and is punishing so many innocent people is intolerable. And so, the evidence has to be internally denied." Denial. That applies to the people of Russia, though they subsist on a diet of lies, and to the supporters of our revered PM who also, it has been proved, is buddies with the untruth.

54.

Grey skies. Gunmetal grey with a touch of AR-15 black.

Nineteen elementary school children and two teachers have been slaughtered in the small town of Uvalde in Texas by eighteen-year-old Salvador Ramos. He entered the school in body armour with a handgun and an AR-15 Assault Rifle. It's the twenty-seventh such shooting this year in America but the message, obvious in nearly every other country in the world, that the fewer guns there are, the safer you will be, fails to register with the gun-owners of America.

Their clarion call is clear and unshaken --'We need guns to protect us.' Presumably against people with guns. There is a fundamental flaw in this thinking which it would be tempting to believe rational people would grasp, but as Donald Trump's rise has demonstrated, reason is not flavour of the month in the grand old US of A. Rather than feel abhorrence at the slaughter of children and begin to question the universal

availability of dangerous weapons, the

answer from the gun-lovers is to arm

teachers.

Attempts have been made over the years

to challenge the Second Amendment, a Bill

passed in Dec 1791 when there were very few

AR-15 Assault rifles about, the latest being a

case in Massachusetts. There would be no

change to the Constitution was the ruling.

Even weapons not in existence at the time of

the Constitution were accepted as meeting the intention of the Founding Fathers.

That an amendment to the Constitution drawn up in 1791 should be treated as sacrosanct seems even more absurd when you find out that two years earlier the French revolted, and that same month six-hundred soldiers were killed by Indians, and Mozart died. Surely even die-hard Republicans can accept that the world has moved on, though events in Washington such as a reprise of the Storming of the Bastille in 1789 might suggest a reversion to more primitive times is on the cards. Reason is not on the side of the gunslingers, but big business certainly is.

The NRA was formed in 1871 by two Civil War veterans to 'promote and encourage rifle shooting on a scientific basis.' Not quite sure what the 'scientific basis' was intended to indicate, other than that even then, they felt they needed a reason for shooting. In 1975 a lobbying arm of the Association was formed— The Institute of Legislative Action, and in 1977 a Political Action Committee was formed to channel funds to affect legislation.

It does seem as if the NRA has been aware of

the need to influence the Powers-that-Be

over the years and in that it has been

successful. The Republican Party, with its

majority in the Senate and its umbilical

attachment to the Second Amendment no

doubt aided by funds from the NRA, with few

exceptions, stands firm against gun-control.

'It's not the guns folks—it's the folk who

shoot them.' An argument that holds no

water when eighteen-year-olds anywhere can

arm themselves with these weapons. In Britain the Dunblane killings in 1996 where sixteen children and their teacher were killed brought about legislation the following year which banned most handguns in private use, made semi-automatic weapons illegal, required shotguns to be licensed and made registration mandatory for all gunowners. Since Dunblane there has only been one shooting in Britain, in Cumbria in 2010 where twelve people were killed. Two killings in twenty-six years in Britain twenty-seven killings in America, in five months. Five times the population still doesn't hold water.

A research paper in 2017 found that for every one hundred people in Britain there were 5.3 guns. That same year in America the number was 120.5 guns. Of course, those that blame the shooter and not the weapon have a point. It's not rational people who massacre others, it's people with mental health issues or personal grievances that transcend normal resolution. But the fact remains, in any society there are going to be people with mental health issues. If those people are denied the use of weapons, then mass killing will be made more unlikely. America, or perhaps more accurately, The Republican Party and the NRA need to clamber over the centuries since The Second Amendment was ratified and accept the reality of the results of mass gun-ownership. There is only one logical outcome to the notion that if you're afraid of your neighbour because he has a gun, then you must arm yourself. You must protect yourself because that's your right.

Against what? Well, against folk with guns of course. But supposing neither of us had... No, don't go there. Just don't—we're the NRA.

Perhaps if God had wanted us to have guns, he'd have given Adam one and then Eve. And he'd have prayed to Himself that neither had mental health issues.

As a post-script to the Uvalde shooting, Canada has announced a ban on the sale and transfer of handguns. Not bound by a constitution that endorses gun-ownership, Canada has shown a more grown-up attitude to gun ownership. In 2020 Laws were passed placing bans on 1,500 types of miliary style firearms. Gun licenses were revoked of those involved in domestic violence or harassment and the modification of magazines was criminalised. Magazines must hold no more than five rounds. For a while, Canada has had stringent gun-control rules. Background checks, courses and testing are all deemed necessary before owning a gun, yet gun violence has been on the increase. One of the key difficulties for the Canadian Government has, and no doubt will be the smuggling of firearms from America. We can but hope that the U.S.A. will observe Canada's efforts and see them as a lesson to be learned.

55.

The garden full of birds. Izzy very annoyed by the intruders. Sky puffy with clouds.

The NATION is stirring. The Monarch has been on the throne for seventy years...

Nostalgia, unlike neuralgia can be very calming. Nostos and algos—in the Greek, home and pain got married to produce nostalgia, the pain of the present comforted by remembrance of home, of the past. Great Britain today is a place of some pain to many. People are eating their children to survive or farting on their log-fires to keep them going. Russians are stopping us from eating our Weetabix and we have a PM who is called a liar to his face by interviewers and merely responds by saying he disagrees. He's a bit of a rogue. No wonder we feel nostalgic for better times. The issue is, were they better times, or have the times always been a bit shit?

The catalyst for this current outbreak of nostalgia is the Queen's Platitude Jubilee. Our wee monarch (an oasis of stability in a changing world—is that good?) has been on the throne for seventy years which is a long time to be sitting anywhere much less on a throne. Every night there are TV programmes whipping us into a frenzy of Royal love by showing the Queen's home videos, which

reveal just how like us this family were.

We see them cavort in the heather at

Glass-allt-shiel, the lodge built by Queen

Victoria near Lochnagar; we see the young

queen skipping, and we see her stroking her

corgis. We watch the family—yes, they're a

family just like yours, well, almost— picnicking

by the loch, the King her dad in his plus-fours

because that's what you must wear when

you're in Scottishland. later we see the queen

as a young girl on the family's boat larking

about in warmer climes on their way to visit their subjects. Now, let's not get too satirical about all this home video stuff. I've rarely watched a home video that didn't make the participants look foolish by their self-conscious antics. No, that's not the point, really. The point is, we are fixated on our Monarch in this time of trouble and want to look back.

The Union Jack factories will be in overdrive as they produce flags and bunting for the street parties to celebrate sitting on a throne for seventy years. And let's face it, if ever Union Jack was in trouble, it's now. The

people of Northern Ireland have elected a Sinn

Fein president and the people of Scotland are

not enamoured of The Conservative Party nor

even of a little woman who has sat on a throne

in England for Seventy years. Unless you live

in Ballater of course, where the Royals are

thought of as the neighbours up the road who

are happy to Royal Appoint butchers and

bakers for supplying sausages and rowies to

Balmoral.

But let's get back to nostalgia and a Britain of the past.

The Commonwealth, that institution of Empire that was never far from The Queen's Speech every Christmas still exists as a group of post-colonial territories some of which still want the Queen to be regarded as their Head of State. In today's world however cracks are appearing in the ties with The Motherland and foreign trips by The Royal Family are as likely to produce boos as they are to initiate a hysteria of flag waving from Primary School pupils given a day off school.

Of the fifty-four nations that constitute The Commonwealth, only fifteen still regard The Queen as Head of State and it should be said some of these 'nations' have populations smaller than post codes in London. One wonders what St Kitts and Nevis gets out of all this. The Caribbean nations, post Black Lives Matter have woken up after a long sleep to the notion that they are paying obeisance to a white family who process through crowded streets in their land-rover every few years to

show how grateful they are for all the

sugarcane. Barbados wants an apology for

slavery. Fat chance. Nevertheless,

miraculously, The Commonwealth survives,

and its countries form a third of the World's

landmass. What benefits come from

membership seem elusive and Britain's trade

with Commonwealth countries is much the

same as our trade with Germany—eight

percent, not an overwhelming statistic.

Flags, bunting and street parties to celebrate our Queen's longevity and throne-sitting provide a suitable diversion from Corn-mop's travails. Brexit's benefits still wait to be discovered however (Reece-Mogg will fix it) and our decision to leave the club and the subsequent Covid pandemic have left Britannia struggling to replace the trading benefits of EU membership. Nostalgia kicks in as we watch footage of the young queen and associate her doings with our own— "Oh, that was in 1952 and while she's in 'Treetops' in

Kenya— going up the fig tree a princess—and coming down a queen, I was just a wee boy on my bike almost being run over by a ten-ton truck. Isn't life wonderful.'" Well, it is if you can look back rather than forward and looking back is a shaky video where folk make faces and smile royally. Come to think of it, I wouldn't mind seeing a video of young Boris cavorting in Central Park. I wonder if there might be footage of him telling papa how much he wants to be King of the World while he steps on the neck of a ragamuffin. Well, that's work

in progress, my son.

56.

A blustery day where sun and cloud vie for

dominance. Neither is winning.

The adage 'Old age doesn't come by itself'

has always painted a picture for me of an old

man approaching along with his friends Ache,

Stoop, Fall, Forget, Regret, Rage and a host of

other buddies in tow. Oscar Wilde noted that

'the tragedy of growing old is not that one is

old but that one is young.' and of course, (as

usual) he was right. The face and the body

sink but if you're lucky the mind can still float.

As we see more and more centenarians in our

society what strikes one is how 'alive' some of

them are, how their old faces can still smile as

the spirit remains undimmed. I suppose there

are a few who don't smile but have still clung

on to life with a shake of the head at what the

world has become, but they are rare. There

seems little doubt that a 'positive' outlook on

life can extend it, but as I age myself, I find it

increasingly difficult to imagine the world in fifty

years' time let alone one hundred.

This year of our Lord (whoever she is) 2022, like old age, brings not just days but a host of hangers-on. There have been times when nothing of much significance happens, but these days every hour seems to bring a host of happenings.

Covid is still with us but has been contained by vaccination as flu has been. It's to be hoped that the experiences of the last two years have alerted virologists to the need for a world-wide consensus on how to co-operate to control future pandemics. The death toll in our Care-homes was a chilling lesson on how a virus can afflict those not in robust health and Governments on how to balance 'business' with 'public health.' Now we are paying for the pandemic both financially and in human terms as many people who lost their jobs have discovered new and less onerous ways of making a living. But that's only one of today's accoutrements, for days don't come by themselves—another is the daily reports of the war in Europe.

Russia's blockade of the Black Sea ports is in danger of causing famine in countries such as Egypt, Lebanon and Pakistan. Ukraine's grain silos are full, and the next harvest is only weeks away. Without storage it will rot in the fields. Meanwhile Putin has learned to concentrate his points of attack and his forces make gains in the East as Ukraine pleads for more weapons. Disunity stalks the air.

America's President Biden talks the talk on Ukraine and sends weapons with the proviso that the long-range missile systems should not be used to send missiles into Russian territory.

Naturally, Ukraine accepts this. But isn't it odd

that a country under attack is prevented from

attacking its aggressor? What happened to the

axiom 'attack is the best form of defence?' Oh,

I forgot, Russia wouldn't like it. NATO stands

on the sidelines of this war with conventional

forces many times more effective than

Russia's but in the shape of a 'peaceful' club.

One can't help feeling that in the face of

Putin's aggression NATO is a big nun facing a

small mugger with a gun. This mugger

however doesn't want money, he wants

territory, and this nun doesn't know how to

respond, never having been mugged before.

The analogy ends there however, for the

NATO club has dissident members. Unity of

purpose is shaky at best, as Germany, France,

Hungary and Turkey each plays the NIMBY

card. Orban and Erdogan are mini Putins and

reluctant to commit to ousting a leader like

themselves. Germany has gas and oil issues

and is reluctant to cut essential supplies which

would seriously affect its economy. President

Macron has expressed the view that Russia should not be humiliated in Ukraine, a stance that many have seen as subverting NATO and the EU's efforts. But France has provided Aid and weapons to Ukraine, and perhaps Macron has history on his side when he suggests a solution acceptable to both sides. Germany's humiliation after the Treaty of Versailles in 1919 was one which encouraged the ex-soldier Adolf Hitler in his rise to power. And Putin's desire to re-establish some semblance of a Russian Empire is based on his self-confessed hatred of Gorbachev's decision to

dismantle The USSR in Dec 1991. However,

it's difficult to see Macron's desire to avoid

humiliation for Russia in any other terms than

Ukraine's ceding of The Donbas. Does Macron

really believe that Putin would be happy with

this? Chechnya, Crimea, The Donbas…why

stop there when you can still threaten nuclear

war should NATO interfere with your

ambitions? While the bully raises his hammer

and threatens, do we shy away with our

hammer lowered and wait for him to die or do

we raise it and watch his eyes? 'Do you feel lucky, Putin?' As Clint would put it. The war in Ukraine could not have come at a worse time (if war can ever be said to come at a good time) for the world.

With the shortage of oil and gas comes the need to replace Russian exports to Western Europe with our own energy production. At a time when the baked meats of Cop 26 in Glasgow are still warm, we see new oil and coal fields being opened across the globe. Targets become meaningless in the face of necessity while the pole melts and the bears

lose the knowledge of what a seal looks like.

Days come not by themselves but with the

pain that being human brings. Keep smiling,

the carers, the nurses, the doctors, the aid

workers, the mothers holding their children, the

good guys and girls, for you will last longer.

Would that I could believe 'the meek will inherit

the Earth.'

57.

Grey again above. One of these days summer will remember to come.

An appearance by one of the 'old' Tories in The Observer today. Chris Patten writing about his days as Governor of Hong Kong in his Diaries. Particularly interested on his take on the present Conservative Government which he sees as 'an English nationalist party which is populist, but fatally—without being popular.' He argues that it becomes more difficult to talk to regimes such as China from a moral standpoint when here at home the Government threatens democratic norms such as proroguing Parliament, undermining the independence of the Judiciary and the neutrality of the Civil Service, and threatening to ignore the Northern Ireland Protocol.

'Populist' is a term normally applied to a politician who sets him or herself as the voice of 'the People' against the elite, or conventional Government and who

characteristically wages a constant battle

against forces which are said to be thwarting

the will of 'the people.' It's a present for a

Trump who waged a war against the media

and the Washington Elite. Trump's ability to

act as 'one of you' was laughable to those

wise enough to see in this multi-billionaire

businessman one of rich elite himself. His use

of the term 'fake news' to trash any criticism

again was his dishing of what he characterised

as an intellectual plot to undermine the

people's will. 'They hate me because I'm with you' works. Washington politics was 'the swamp' and he was going to drain it. And he pulled it off, as did and do numerous other populist leaders. The rub is of course, that if you set yourself up to upturn the establishment applecart, you then make your own applecart and that's the problem. Even today as a committee examine the invasion of The Capitol (a committee with no punitive powers), it's unlikely that he will be prosecuted for what happened that day. The man was populist and is still popular and that is America's problem.

Corn-mop's 'Get Brexit Done' was a rallying

cry to middle England who were convinced

that their woes were attributable to

membership of the E.U. and its open borders.

A majority of eighty MP's swept into the

Commons and the rest is history. Patten

questions Corn-mop's enduring popularity and

he's probably right, but perhaps that's

attributable to his promises over Brexit and the

'cheeky chappy' grin that rarely leaves his

countenance. The most effective leaders are

those whose integrity guides them rather than the scam that they represent the 'ordinary people.' Patten says he tried to explain to his opposite number in Beijing 'what the rule of law was, that it wasn't rule by law.'

The terms 'fazhi' and 'renzhi' define the differences in how 'law' is applied in a society. In China 'fazhi' or rule by law enables the ruling administration to set the laws by which the country is ruled. 'Renzhi' or rule of law is effected when the laws of a country limit the powers of the rulers. Interesting that Patten's opposite number didn't quite get it, but why would he? The young Chinese concert pianist Yuja Wang, talking about her parents, made the point that in China 'You work for the common welfare rather than for the individual. Working for the individual is almost synonymous with being selfish.' I'm sure Patten understood this but like the rest of us in The West we mistrust the efficacy of this approach to society. Thatcher's comment about Society comes to mind. Perhaps the altruistic nature of this seems on paper to be worthy, but the power it invests in its rulers

opens the door to corruption. Just look at

Putin, or Erdogan, or Bolsonaro, or Orban.

Power corrupts and absolute power corrupts

absolutely. Rule by law is a suit they all want

to wear.

58.

Blue sky and warm. Summer at last.

No trains, North of Glasgow. Clearly if you're a government with no policies what you must do to get support is to create enemies. Plenty of opponents of the Rwanda deportation scheme including all the Bishops in the Church of England. If you take your moral guidance from these chaps then you should be opposed to the scheme, that is unless you're a Brexit voter and hung up on the conviction that immigration is the source of our ills. If you are going to be inconvenienced by the Rail Strike, then you will probably be opposed to it and demand that the rail workers go back to work. What do you care if their wages are far below inflation; what do you care if the median salary quoted by politicians is a lie? It's every working man for himself. Isn't it?

Setting up groups of workers to be vilified worked for Thatcher but this time numerous public sector workers are on the warpath: Police, Teachers, Solicitors and more, while Corn-mop buys his season ticket to Kyiv, keeping well clear of Wakefield and Tiverton where Tory massacres are about to take place. Custer should have avoided The Big Horn by rushing home to see Libby about the kitchen extension. Difficult to avoid the thought that defeat for the railmen will mean defeat for a host of other public sector employees. My own experience as a teacher in the eighties was a simple one—if you don't fight you don't get and don't expect sympathy from other sectors of the population who are only concerned with the inconvenience your action has caused them. The Tory Party has no respect for workers whom they regard as out-with the profit-making economy. Wage caps year after year leave these groups trailing behind the Private Sector many of whom receive bonuses in addition to salaries.

Reading Jonathan Freedland's book 'The Escape Artist' about the escape from Auschwitz 11(Birkenau) Concentration Camp of Walter Rosenberg I was pulled up short by the term used to describe the sorting of Jews as 'special treatment.' It was also the term used by the Germans in Katowice to indicate Poles who should be executed and the SonderKommando of the camps. 'Sonder' meaning 'special' in German. Interesting that Putin describes the invasion of Ukraine as a 'special military operation.' The word 'special' seems to be a convenient way of describing an act known to its perpetrator to be morally repugnant but a convenient identifier in its vagueness—the ultimate euphemism for savagery made acceptable.

59.

Sunny and warm but a chill wind blows for American women.

In the case of Dogma versus Pragmatism, The Supreme Court of America has ruled there is no constitutional right to abortion in the USA, a decision met with despair by vast swathes of women. This is a right that has existed for nearly fifty years during which time women have had the right to terminate their pregnancies. The Court's Conservative justices, on a path surely to impose the Christian Right's moral convictions on the population, have succeeded in their task.

Justices Gorsuch, Kavanagh and Barrett were all nominated by Donald Trump and their views on abortion were 'pro-life'—that's the life of the child, of course—the mother can go hang. While the men when questioned pre-election were evasive, Barrett, the last to be nominated, made her view clear before appointment. These Justices have now passed a law which in effect takes away a woman's freedom to decide what control she has over her own body. If we imagined Trump was a ghost from the past, we now know that in his wake his machinations remain a clear and present danger to the freedom of many Americans. Judges are in post for life and the decisions they make, incontrovertibly coloured by religious convictions as these are, are being imposed on people who do not hold these views. The Roe versus Wade ruling of 1973 gave general protection to a woman who wished to have an abortion. Now that protection has been taken away, and in many states, abortion will be a criminal offence. If we imagined American gun laws (or the lack of them) to be a throwback to The Wild West (and the Justices have ruled that carrying a concealed weapon 'for defence' should be legal in New York,) this is surely another throwback to a time before enlightenment.

Commentators are already predicting a backlash in the November Congressional elections when women will have the opportunity to vote in Democrat senators who respect women's rights. I wrote earlier about the distinction between The Rule of Law and The Rule by Law. If the Supreme Court makes pronouncements on topics such as trans-rights, or contraception or the rights of other minority groups as they have on abortion, America is in danger of 'rule by law' rather than 'rule of law.' When the minority Christian Right's Justices hold sway over the decisions of The Supreme

Court, we may expect their personal prejudices to take precedence over the common good. Sharia law comes to Washington. Good luck, America.

60.

I once thought the Labour Party stood firmly for the rights of working people. Perhaps they once did, but no longer it seems. David Lammy, The Shadow Secretary of State*, interviewed on TV this morning and asked if he supported the BA workers strike—a group whose pay was reduced by 10% during the pandemic and who now want that pay restored instead of a one-off bonus—said 'No.' No, a Labour shadow minister does not support a group of workers fighting to have their wages restored.

What then does this Party stand for? It stands for avoiding upsetting people that might vote for it. Is that a policy? The more I watch the political shenanigans taking place in England, the more I'm drawn to an Independent Scotland. When you are living with a dangerously irrational person, you need to extricate yourself.

I notice a new tactic emerging from employers: we'll give you a lump sum guys in place of a pay rise. Once you've accepted that, we'll be off the hook and next year you'll be back paid as you were. Sorted.

Corn-mop, the jolly international statesman, flits from country to country like an overweight bee heavy with bags of pollen sorting things out while his hive disintegrates. He says he'll be in office for another two terms. The Labour Party should be having a party, but no, they want him out. Does it occur to them that someone with a smidgeon more integrity might succeed him and re-attract

Tory voters? No. Nuff said. Iraq did for this lot, and they've never found themselves since.

*PS. Three days later Lammy has claimed he misheard the question over the BA pay dispute. He hadn't realised that their pay had been cut by 10% last year. He'd thought they just wanted a 10% increase. Does this man read the papers?

61.

Grey skies as the Atlantic pisses on us.

Six months of Ukrainian turmoil and the rest of

Europe mutters about the cost of everything.

Putin's assault continues to gain ground in The

Donbas. The Black Sea is mined and without

wheat Africa faces starvation. Threats now from Russia towards the Lithuanians who have bravely banned the transit of EU sanctioned goods to Kaliningrad, the city within its borders given to the then Soviet Union at The Potsdam Conference in 1945. Lithuania is a NATO member.

Given NATO's supine response to the invasion of Ukraine, one wonders what pressure it will put on Lithuania to defuse this situation.

Two issues are approaching it seems. One: will Russia stop at the borders of the Donbas, or will they be encouraged to continue towards Kyiv? Two: if Ukraine refuses to accept any peace terms, will the countries of Western Europe continue to supply arms, or will they consider the economic price of the war continuing to be too high? Should they choose the latter, then Putin will have won, Ukraine will be a part of Russia and he can prepare for his next venture in the knowledge that European harmony is a guitar played with two strings. After the Thermopylae that is Ukraine, Xerxes Putin will capture Greece.

62.

Is that the sun? Too early. It always clouds over when the sun gets up early.

I've just seen something remarkable: no, it wasn't Putin donating a kidney to Zelenskyy, or Boris Johnson being truthful, it was Anthony Hopkins on the back page of The Sunday Times 'Style' mag dressed in a long black number with far too many buttons and wearing very funny trainers. He was being an icon of cool or something. It shocked me, but it shouldn't have. If I thought he was taking the piss out of the High Fashion Industry, I could laugh with him, but I'm not sure he wasn't being serious. The man is eighty-four years old and while succumbing to old age is not to be recommended, dressing like a refugee from Star-trek who has bought a pair of trainers a blind man wouldn't wear is not raging against the dying of the light. No, it shouldn't have shocked me, for he was earning money, and that's what you do isn't it, no matter what you must do to earn it. Pity is, I thought he was well-off anyway, and didn't really need to look like a twit for a few quid extra. Come to think of it, is there ever a point when the fabulously rich say to themselves—that's it, I've got enough now.

Of course, this is what you get when you read this magazine—a nose against the glass to peep into the world of the rich and shameless. I was going to write 'mindless' but it's not that, it's a moral issue bathing in money while all around struggle to make ends meet. My problem is I have difficulty forgetting poverty when the rich are smirking in my face. While Ukraine burns, and vast numbers of households here in Britain visit food banks, the Sunday Times readers turn the pages of this obscene mag and speculate how reasonable that long white dress is at only £6,600.

Truly. Or perhaps a nice beach basket for only

£400. This isn't about 'style' it's about

conspicuous consumerism in a society in the

throes of want, and it is to my mind, obscene.

63. Grey skies with occasional showers. Gloom with even gloomier moments.

Coming towards the end of my six months journal and not much has changed. The war in Ukraine rages on while the EU, NATO and President Biden fumble their way from summit to summit feigning a specious unity. The only concrete agreement is to talk of unity and chuck weapons into Ukraine for the Ukrainians to fight it out with Putin.

Is this the first time in history that an invaded State has been forbidden from inflicting any military harm on the territory of the invader? 'We'll give you long range missiles,' said Biden 'but you must promise not to fire them into Russia.' Of course, Zelenskyy agrees. What choice does he have? It's to be hoped that agreements to bolster NATO forces in The Baltic go ahead, and that any peace agreement over Ukraine does not send Europe to sleep again listening to Putin's lullaby's. 'That's the special operation completed folks, can we get back to a bit of peaceful money-laundering and cyber warfare please. You know you want to.'

But the war has taken our eyes off the most pressing issue facing mankind—global warming. As the clock ticks towards a rise in temperature of 1.5 degrees plus, the energy crisis has encouraged France, Germany, Britain and China, to re-open or create new fossil-fuel developments. Cop26 seems a vague memory of promises and vows that will never be kept. Alaskan glaciers are melting, and sea-rise is an inevitable consequence which will inundate islands in the Pacific. Where will these people go to save themselves? For if it's not water that threatens, it's drought.

There is a growing migration surge from Africa, South America and the Middle East, as conflict, political upheaval and climate change forces people to seek a better life, but the rich industrial countries have failed to come to terms with the inevitable and continue to battle against migrants. Canute couldn't stop the tide, and neither can walls, wire, or Rwanda. What is required is a global acknowledgment that there is going to be a population drift North in the coming decades and some means of accommodating this is essential.

———————————

Six months of turmoil ending for this journal. Covid still with us. The conflict in Ukraine still with us. Global Warming still with us and worsening. The British political system still in turmoil as a new PM is in process of being elected. America divided. This may have been six months that changed the world but plus ça change, plus c'est la m me chose. We must be optimistic, however, that good sense and the instinct to survive will tell in the end.

A heat wave coming from the South.

Printed in Great Britain
by Amazon

85309465R00251